STREAMING CULTURE

SocietyNow

SocietyNow: short, informed books, explaining why our world is the way it is, now.

The SocietyNow series provides readers with a definitive snapshot of the events, phenomena and issues that are defining our 21st century world. Written leading experts in their fields, and publishing as each subject is being contemplated across the globe, titles in the series offer a thoughtful, concise and rapid response to the major political and economic events and social and cultural trends of our time.

SocietyNow makes the best of academic expertise accessible to a wider audience, to help readers untangle the complexities of each topic and make sense of our world the way it is, now.

Poverty in Britain: Causes, Consequences and Myths
Tracy Shildrick

The Trump Phenomenon: How the Politics of Populism Won in 2016
Peter Kivisto

Becoming Digital: Towards a Post-Internet Society
Vincent Mosco

Understanding Brexit: Why Britain Voted to Leave the European Union
Graham Taylor

Selfies: Why We Love (and Hate) Them
Katrin Tiidenberg

Internet Celebrity: Understanding Fame Online
Crystal Abidin

impacts. Loaded with examples that will speak to every audience, Arditi has produced a text that is astonishing in its depth and breadth and is essential for understanding a modern digital society.

With *Streaming Culture*, David Arditi provides an engaging blueprint for understanding the expansive impact of streaming services. Theoretically rich, historically grounded, and full of examples from a range of media forms, Arditi offers fresh insights into how streaming platforms are reshaping media culture.

STREAMING CULTURE

Subscription Platforms and the Unending Consumption of Culture

BY

DAVID ARDITI

University of Texas at Arlington, USA

United Kingdom – North America – Japan – India
Malaysia – China

Emerald Publishing Limited
Howard House, Wagon Lane, Bingley BD16 1WA, UK

First edition 2021

Copyright © 2021 David Arditi
Published under exclusive licence by Emerald Publishing Limited.

Reprints and permissions service
Contact: permissions@emeraldinsight.com

British Library Cataloguing in Publication Data
A catalogue record for this book is available from the British Library

ISBN: 978-1-83982-773-0 (Print)
ISBN: 978-1-83982-768-6 (Online)
ISBN: 978-1-83982-772-3 (Epub)

ISOQAR certified
Management System,
awarded to Emerald
for adherence to
Environmental
standard
ISO 14001:2004.

Certificate Number 1985
ISO 14001

INVESTOR IN PEOPLE

CONTENTS

1

INTRODUCTION: CAUGHT IN THE STREAM

On the first day of my Introduction to Popular Culture course, I always ask my students the same question: what is your favorite part of popular culture? In the fall of 2014, I was surprised when 10 students responded "YouTube." It shouldn't have been surprising, but in my mind, YouTube remained a means to consume other areas of popular culture. However, to my students the mix of streamed culture on the popular video sharing platform pointed to a cultural form in-and-of itself. For them, YouTube is not just a place to stream hand-me-down culture, but a site of novel cultural production in its own right. Streaming culture is both a noun and a verb (discussed further below). As a noun, streaming culture refers to the cultural practices surrounding websites like YouTube. As a verb, streaming culture speaks to the act of consuming culture using internet and communication technologies. My students identify with streaming culture as a quintessential aspect of popular culture.

Streaming culture changed the way that I teach Introduction to Popular Culture because it enabled me to quickly engage with things that I've never seen myself. Later in the same semester, these students introduced me to "Alex from Target." The simple picture of a kid bagging items at Target became a meme, viewed by millions. After searching for "Alex from Target," we streamed Ellen DeGeneres' interview of him. While no one could explain the attraction to Alex, we were able to witness his 15 minutes of fame. While a photographic meme, "Alex from Target" displays all of the qualities of streaming culture (defined below).

Then came Danielle Bregoli, at the time known as "Cash Me Outside Girl" to my students, in 2016. I'd never heard of her, but they encouraged me to look her up. We watched as a class as Bregoli berated Dr. Phil's studio audience to "cash" her outside. Her taunting was universally streamed by my students before I ever heard of her. The out-of-control teen had millions of people mocking her worldwide—note: cyberbullying is part of streaming culture. Now in 2020, Bregoli is a rapper by the stage name of Bhad Bhabie. Streaming culture allows Bregoli to "cash in" on "cash me outside." People stream her music on Spotify, videos on YouTube, remix her songs on TikTok, and watch her reality TV show on Snapchat. We don't know if people listen to her raps because they think she's the jam or to mock her. The fact is, it doesn't matter which one is the case because Atlantic Records, Warner Brothers Music Group, and Bhad Bhabie cash in on hundreds of millions of streams across digital platforms regardless.

Of course, none of this is surprising. YouTube has been a part of my own cultural imaginary since I worked on my Master's. From bandmates uploading videos of themselves playing guitar to friends sending me videos like "Evolution of Dance." YouTube has been both a site of "sharing" (a term wildly popularized in digital culture, discussed in Chapter 2) and production. Perhaps I didn't think of YouTube as a type of popular culture because it always stood as a place for consuming other types of popular culture. It is a site of participatory culture— "in which fans and other consumers are invited to actively participate in the creation and circulation of new content."[1] Thinking in terms of participatory culture, YouTube seems like just another way for users to share videos. But with the world of vloggers (i.e. video bloggers), comedians, musicians, skaters, and filmmakers who all produce content specifically for YouTube, clearly, YouTube is a type of popular culture.

The cultural world is at our fingertips. Much like my experiences in my Introduction to Popular Culture class, I increasingly find myself looking up obscure pop culture references. Not only can I find answers to my inquiries online, but I can view the content! This is a massive change from the early Internet when it took time for people to write about their cultural obsessions on the web and for others to find them. Over time, the content available has snowballed as people move from one obsession to the next and their content remains available, potentially forever. As a result, now you can find a wiki, blog, or website on just about everything.

A wiki is a website that allows users to edit content collaboratively. Wikis enable users to update content on a given subject. While many have claimed that the Internet brings democracy, wiki technology provides one of the few examples of a democratized web.[2] They allow collectives of people to act like hive minds. If one person creates a website, the content will be limited, but through wikis, anyone who knows something or has a thought about a subject can edit the content. While Wikipedia is the most notorious wiki where people update encyclopedic information about everything, wikis are available in any number of forms from Genius (a lyrics database that allows users to comment and interpret lyrics) to WikiHow (a how-to database where users upload videos and instructions on different tasks).

Blogs, on the other hand, are regularly updated websites that list their content in order with the most recent at the top of the page.[3] Anyone can create a webpage using a blog platform without any idea how to code, which makes this platform widely accessible. Popular blog platforms include Wordpress and Blogger, which are designed for the amateur blogger. The explosion of blogs and wikis enables anyone to upload content to the web—in many instances, content only the uploaders find interesting. While this means the world of information is at our fingertips, it also can have distinct effects on culture.

In summer 2019, my wife and I began binge-watching *Game of Thrones* (I cover binge-watching extensively in Chapter 5). We were terribly late to the show and neither of us read the books by George R.R. Martin. As we watched, I felt completely lost about places and people in the show. However, I could easily search the Internet for a topic and read multiple *Game of Thrones* wikis, which explain all types of relationships and histories of the story-line. Unfortunately, there is a downside. As I found myself looking up details that I didn't fully understand, I also saw spoilers. All of the information at my fingertips also means ALL of the information without chronological considerations. Streaming enables us to watch a television series like one really long movie, but it also has the potential of spoiling the ending and details.

None of this was available in the 1990s. In 1995, Windows 95 changed the way we interact with computers by simplifying a computer's operating system interface. However, most people logged on the Internet using a 28.8 kbps modem, usually through an Internet Service Provider (ISP) such as AOL or Prodigy. The ISP played an outsized role connecting users to information before the widespread use of independent web browsers (ex. Netscape Navigator). The early Internet did not work well for multimedia content. I recall clicking on webpages (that were difficult to navigate) and waiting for images to load. Sometimes people had too much fun with their websites and had fireworks or cascading stars on entry—this slowed down the page exponentially. It's hard to imagine now, but it was really difficult to find what you were looking for on the web and if you were lucky enough to find something, you had to wait forever to view it. Streaming video was next to impossible in the 1990s. Yahoo seemed revolutionary to me in both its search and cataloging functionality. But finding information remained difficult until I discovered Google.

If *Game of Thrones* was around in 1995, my experience would have been entirely different. First, if I did not watch it from the beginning, I would have had to wait to purchase (or rent) the VHS tapes. The entire series would take up a shelf on a bookcase. If I missed an episode in the original broadcast, I would have been out-of-luck. There is a chance that I could have made up random episodes through reruns, but even that would mean watching the episodes out of order. Second, when we started watching the tapes, I would have been unable to bring myself up to speed on the details of the show. On the outside chance that I found an obsessive fan who documented the characters, places and histories of Westeros (the fictional land the story takes place), I would have had a difficult time loading the pages. Finally, while I am not a member of any *Game of Thrones* groups, I know that today I could become part of a virtual community of fans. In 1995, I would have been on my own with no easy way to build community around the show.

From Blogger to YouTube and Amazon Prime to Netflix, these platforms changed the way we consume culture and the cultures that arise alongside platforms. The point of this book isn't to provide a normative value judgement about streaming services, but rather, to demonstrate how things changed and infer the consequences of these changes. Streaming is part of our everyday lives, and that isn't likely to change anytime soon. We must begin to interrogate streaming culture. How does streaming change our lives? What is streaming culture? What is different between streaming culture and downloading culture or analog culture? Why does streaming culture matter? As this book suggests, streaming culture matters because it fundamentally transforms the way we consume culture and the fundamental structure of capitalism.

CULTURE

Culture is an ambiguous term that suffers from its ubiquity. In this book, I use a "Cultural Studies" approach to the term. In that sense, culture is the process through which people make symbolic meaning out of everyday things.[4] We make meaning through a shared understanding of symbols. These symbols can be words, signs, or objects. We interpret these symbols individually and collectively. Symbols come to possess meaning only because we exist within communities. In more traditional senses of the term culture, these communities are cultures. I shy away from labelling communities as cultures because of the emphasis on process in my definition and to productively distinguish terminology. Through our interactions with other people, our understanding of a given symbol can change over time and in a specific context. The communities themselves remain fluid. As a member of one community, I may see something one way, but as a member of a parallel community, I may be able to see it a different way. We have no direct control over the changing meanings of symbols. Culture is not static, and as we interact with others, meanings change.

Furthermore, as literary theorist Raymond Williams states: "Culture is ordinary."[5] We do not need to go to a special place (museum, concert hall, theater, etc.) to experience culture. Culture is everywhere in our everyday lives. This declaration that culture is ordinary distinguishes it from the notion of "high" culture. A classical conception of culture is that it must be learned. Thinking about culture as learned means that only the wealthy have access to it—to be cultured. People need a special education to appreciate opera or abstract art. But if culture is ordinary, it is part of our everyday lives. In the role that different cultural objects play in our lives, no difference exists between opera and someone playing a guitar around a campfire, Picasso and graffiti, or Shakespeare and HowTo-Basic. It may seem that the first term in each pairing in the previous sentence is qualitatively better than the second term, but this is a social judgment not devoid of race, class, and gender inflections. And only time will tell if the creator of HowToBasic becomes as canonical as William Shakespeare, both creators produce boisterous comedy of their respective time period. The point is that these cultural artifacts help us to make meaning out of the world around us, and everyone has access to it.

Some cultural theorists popularized the concept of the circuit of culture.[6] The idea is that there is a constant relationship between cultural consumption, production, representation, identity, and regulation. These unique sites of culture happen together without us thinking much about them. When a television writer works on a script, their identity influences how they construct representations and how they perceive audiences will consume their product. At the same time, the available technologies, dominant media, and policies on content change what the writer will produce. For instance, a television producer may want to produce a show in 4k Ultra HD. However, they come to find out that most of their audience members continue to use regular HD. As a result, they shoot the show in regular HD. After a few years, imagine that there is a huge move to 4k Ultra, but the show cannot be reshot. On the one hand, the technology of what people use to consume the television show affects the way that the show exists in the world. On the other hand, the decisions about the technology to use reflects underlying social conditions. Streaming culture interfaces with each part of the circuit of culture to change the way we interact with media.

The production and consumption of cultural messages are always complex and disputed. Cultural theorist Stuart Hall described the process of encoding/decoding popular culture messages.[7] While the processes remain discreet, they never occur independently from each other. As symbols bounce through the circuit, the dominant cultural order tends to have a determining power over the decoded message in the end.[8] An example that I always give my students comes from the 2012 American presidential election. A journalist asked Ann Romney (GOP candidate Mitt Romney's wife) her favorite television show. She responded *Modern Family*[9]—a sitcom that emphasized non-normative familial situations. In response, one of the show's creators tweeted "We'll offer her the role of officiant at Mitch & Cam's wedding. As soon as its legal."[10] The punch line is that creators designed *Modern Family* to critique the very so-called "traditional" values that Romney espouses. However, the dominant reading of *Modern Family* allows people to believe that these non-normative values are funny, not serious. As a result, and according to one reading, the creators of *Modern Family* actually reinforce conceptions of a "traditional" family. Of course, the message can be decoded differently; for instance, to normalize same-sex relationships as well as intergenerational and cross-cultural unions. Cultural texts, no matter how transgressive, operate within a dominant cultural context, while never losing the potential to challenge and transgress dominant cultural values – after all same-sex marriage *is* now legal. The dominant cultural context informs every part of the circuit of culture, and we're really just along for the ride.

In this book, I explore two senses of culture. On the one hand, the culture that we consume. The videos, music, video games, and software that we engage through digital networks. On the other hand, the culture that we identify with in that consumption—the networks of people and the symbolic meaning we create. The way that we make meanings out of the videos, music, video games, software with the people with whom we consume them. The relationship between these two senses of the term culture create streaming culture. Each chapter addresses both aspects of culture applied to a different media. People don't just stream videos on their phones, they send them to their friends, share on social media, and comment. The context of watching *Friends* on Netflix in 2019 changed from watching it on NBC from 1994-2004. This does not mean that new technologies change culture. Rather, a complex relationship exists between culture and technology. People deploy new technologies in creative ways that bring meaning to the cultural texts.

STREAMING

To stream is to have constant motion, and constant change. Streaming is fleeting and always changing. If you think about a stream of water, the water is in motion. If you drop a leaf on top of a stream, the water carries it down stream quickly. The only constant is that the water moves past you. The stream is ever-changing, much like culture. Culture is streaming. We're only beginning to see the parallels between the two, so in some ways streaming culture is culturing culture because culture is an always changing process. But before I get too far ahead of myself, I want to analyze the technological side of streaming.

As I discussed above, the Internet, in its infancy, did not have the capacity to stream cultural content very well. Slow internet speeds and slow computers made loading an image difficult. Bad search engines made finding what you wanted impossible. The lack of digital content amplified the Internet as a desert for finding movies, films, TV shows, and video games. When you could find something, there was not a technical infrastructure that enabled 24-hour access. With widespread cable modem access and mobile broadband, bandwidth stopped being a barrier to cultural content. Now our cellphones have more computing power than mainframe computers did in 1995. Computer manufacturers make laptop computers available with 1 terabyte hard drives for $280. Roughly 1,000 movies fit on a 1TB hard drive! More importantly, because of so-called Cloud Computing, the 1 terabyte hard drive is often redundant. Why download movies when you can stream them from Netflix or Amazon?

Cloud computing is a euphemism that makes access to digital information seem ephemeral. Because we stream information from the "cloud," it feels as though the information is stored in the sky somewhere. Of course, this could not be further from the truth. The cloud is a series of servers that store data. These servers are massive pollution generating machines that require carbon emitting cooling systems to keep them from burning up. While we think of the cloud as the blue sky, the hardwired server centers create smog. A better definition for cloud computer is "a system that moves data stored on individual computers and in the IT departments of institutions to large, distant data centers operated by companies that charge for storage and use."[11] While we do not store the movies on our local hard drives, they exist on a hard drive somewhere.

Regardless of where cultural content is stored, cloud computing and broadband enable us to access information quickly and remotely. The convergence of these technologies enables streaming. In 2016, a group of researchers mapped Netflix's Content Distribution Network (CDN) across the world.[12] The study identifies 4,669 servers at 243 locations. Netflix's CDN enables the company to provide access to movies and televisions at high-speeds across the world. When we log-on to Netflix to watch a movie, we don't think about the location of these servers, how our distance from them affects our viewing experience, or how many other people are watching the same movie at the same time. All that we know is that we want to watch *Murder Mystery* and turn it on our television. The most typical interruption to our viewing capabilities is an interruption to internet access. The infrastructure that enables streaming vanishes into a black box at the point where the cable enters our modems.

Increasingly, we interact with cultural content through platforms— "digital infrastructures that enable two or more groups to interact."[13] These platforms structure the ways that we can consume cultural content. While we think of platforms as a way to consume culture, we often forget that there are social, technical, economic, and ideological reasons for the construction and performance of each platform. For instance, Netflix started as a mail-order DVD rental platform aimed at competing with Blockbuster. This informs the logic of the subscription model in place on Netflix. Executives at Netflix could change the structure any time, but they tend not to because it would interfere with cultural identifications with the platform and brand. The purpose of this book is to begin thinking about the ways that streaming platforms affect culture.

WHY DOES STREAMING CULTURE MATTER?

There are two points that I want to make clear about streaming culture. First, as we switch to streaming cultural content, we change our interactions with cultural texts. Second, the push to streaming marks a shift in the form of capitalism as large corporations seek to extract more value from commodities. I argue streaming culture matters because corporations deployed it to hook us into cultural consumption in a way that perpetually increases the amount we pay for cultural content.

Interactions with Cultural Texts

Consumption cultures arise from consuming culture. I do not state this from any normative value judgment. The way we consumed culture in an analog world is no better or worse than the way we consume culture today. However, problems exist in the "consumption" part. At the point when we discuss consumption, we commodify culture. Culture wasn't always commodified, and it doesn't have to be commodified.[14] I prefer to refer to cultural use in all its forms (listen, watch, play, do). In fact, streaming enables new ways of interacting with cultural texts that can operate outside of commodification.

From its earliest manifestations, media companies accused streaming platforms of "piracy."[15] While the term piracy does not express an explicit legal doctrine, it invokes a moral panic.[16] Labelling something piracy is a rhetorical strategy that makes the labeled act seem reprehensible if not (necessarily) illegal. While Napster (discussed in Chapter 2) did not stream music the way we think of with Spotify, it did facilitate the stream of digital ones and zeros to personal computers through the Internet. On the early web, people would upload user-recorded videos to their personal websites. There were a number of websites that trafficked in these types of videos. They were of poor quality and quickly taken down when copyright holders learned of these sites. At the same time, internet radio stations facilitated early music streaming. The recording industry did not appreciate internet radio stations, but because a legal structure existed for radio, labels did not call these stations pirates. The piracy argument works by scaring would-be users into different practices at the same time that copyright holders convince policymakers to change policies.[17] Untold streaming practices died before they began as people shied away from specific practices and certain technologies closed following legal actions.

The cultural practice of streaming changes the cultural practice of using cultural content. In the early days of television, neighbors would gather to watch television programming.[18] Then as every home in a neighborhood owned at least one television, people quit going to other people's homes to watch TV. The idyllic form of watching TV became family time, but eventually, each household owned multiple TV sets, which cut down on TV time as family time. Streaming changes these practices further as every screen (TV, phone, tablet, or computer) becomes a site of TV, film, or video watching. Now a family can be gathered in one room with mom watching a broadcast show on the living room television, a daughter using a tablet to watch someone play Fortnite on Twitch, and a son watching TikTok clips on his phone. We went from collective TV watching to individualized watching—structured watching to anarchic watching.

These practices change the basic structure of watching in an inhabited space, but the practices change as well. While the mom watches, she may be following a Twitter hashtag about the show. The daughter may be watching someone play while chatting with others about the game play. The son may be making his own TikTok videos and interacting with his followers. Communities arise out of the consumption of this cultural content. Chuck Tryon calls this "platform mobility. . . encompassing the ongoing shift toward ubiquitous, mobile access to a wide range of entertainment choices."[19] Everyone accessing different content in the same room allows people to construct their own communities. Streaming culture gives rise to these new communities, and contrary to those who would say this causes social isolation, I argue that these interactions increase social interaction—they just may be highly mediated interactions.

Shifting Capitalism

Corporate quest for profits drives streaming culture, especially the subscription variety. Whereas culture stood apart from business interests before the twentieth-century, a remarkable shift took place that emphasizes the commodity logic of culture. The more we stream, the more the Culture Industry creates profit. Culture Industry is a term developed by Max Horkheimer and Theodor Adorno to differentiate cultural consumption from "mass culture."[20] When people began referring to mass culture in the early twentieth-century, Horkheimer and Adorno thought this sounded too much like culture that emerged from the masses. The quintessential example is broadcast radio, which sends a signal out to a largely passive audience. Horkheimer and Adorno viewed mass culture as culture produced from above and forced upon the masses. To distinguish the top-down approach of commodified culture, they called it the Culture Industry—by emphasizing the industrial nature of production they placed its goods alongside other commodities from shoes to cars. In the Culture Industry, we can see the Fordist logic of production at work. Under Fordism (aka, Taylorism), mass production worked by individuating tasks—each worker had one job—and the commodity moved along a conveyor belt on its way to production. Horkheimer and Adorno argued cultural commodities followed the same logic. From Tin Pan Alley in New York City where the modern songwriting system developed to Hollywood and the mass production of film to Motown Records in Detroit, which used assembly line production to make music. These sites of mass cultural production resemble the Fordist logics at work in twentieth-century production. However, we go through distinct phases of capitalism, and streaming cultural commodities marks a new phase. In 2019, it is clear that we've entered a new phase of capitalism: unending consumption.[21]

As capitalism has developed, there have been clear moments of transition from one mode of capitalist organization to another. For instance, industrial capitalism required the mass production of similar goods. Capitalism in general is the endless accumulation of capital by a ruling class and the use of wage labor to produce commodities for capitalists to profit off. Capital is a social relation where labor is congealed in money, land and commodities—capital is not money necessarily. The industrial phase focused on producing more goods. The system hinged on planned obsolescence—industry made sure that their goods had a shelf-life, and periodically, consumers would have to buy newer versions of commodities. However, business owners and corporations recognized that they can only sell so many cars or record players. Take the record player, for instance. People only needed one record player in their home. Record player manufacturers recognized that they could increase sales (and profits) by selling music to play on record players. Each home may have one record player, but they can own dozens of records.

This process of providing more consumer goods is known as the expansion of the means of consumption.[22] Basically, capitalists provide more consumer goods for people with expendable income to consume. The expansion of the means of consumption occurred as a way to reduce overproduction while growing capital. These consumer goods are primarily in the form of cultural commodities. The system worked well to stabilize the global economy, but it requires continual acceleration. Streaming culture accelerates the expansion of the means of consumption. Think about all the things we consume today that we didn't consume 30 years ago: cell phones, internet service, subscriptions to music and video providers, $5 Starbucks drinks, accelerated fashion seasons, surveillance devices, TVs in every room, computers, tablets, etc. But as people buy more cultural goods, they spend less time with each artifact.

Several phases of capitalism led directly to unending consumption. In 1989, Ben Agger termed the phase of capitalism that resulted from the expansion of the means of consumption "fast capitalism."[23] During fast capitalism, the expansion of the means of consumption accelerated in a way that blurred text and real life and favored quantity over quality. These logics were fundamentally Fordist hinging on the mass production of goods. Then Agger described faster capitalism in which the Internet forecloses thought.[24] Contrary to the founding logic of the Internet,[25] this faster capitalism turned the Internet into a giant shopping mall.[26] The more we consume the more we produce, and the more we produce, the more we consume. Jodie Dean discusses "communicative capitalism" in which "contemporary communications media capture their users in intensive and extensive networks of enjoyment, production, and surveillance."[27] These webs of consumption entrap us because we enjoy them. Nick Srnicek calls this moment platform capitalism because "with a long decline in manufacturing profitability, capitalism has turned to data as one way to maintain economic growth and vitality in the face of a sluggish production sector." This sped-up surveillance capitalism that uses data as the engine for growth resembles older forms of capitalism, but sucks consumers further into its consumptive abyss.

It is necessary at the current moment to rethink the stage of capitalism once again as we move out of communicative capitalism. I call the current stage "unending consumption."[28] When we subscribe to music, video, software, or news services, we provide companies with constant and consistent consumption. It is unending because once we subscribe, there is no out. If you want to continue to listen to music, you have to keep subscribing. Or you may subscribe to a digital newspaper and forget that you have a subscription. In both cases, companies count on the constant return of revenue whether or not you actually consume anything. Furthermore, we're experiencing the proliferation of subscription services; now content owners can choose one platform to stream their content, and consumers must subscribe to multiple platforms if they want to consume this content. The on-demand economy made us think about the cost and value of every transaction. We ask, do I really want to pay 99 cents for a song on iTunes or download it from Pirate Bay? When given the opportunity to subscribe, this calculation changes to whether I'd like to receive infinite songs for $9.99/month—the equivalent of ten 99 cent downloads. Streaming technology ensures easy access to consumers through legal means, and by subscribing to these services, we don't think of the cost in the raw way that on-demand services require. Streaming culture puts the world of cultural content at our fingertips.

LAYOUT OF THE BOOK

In sum, the argument of this book is that corporations use streaming technology to change the way we consume culture, which embeds us in a logic of capitalism that forces us to consume more. I call this economy of expanded consumption unending consumption. While we have a finite amount of time to consume cultural commodities in our leisure time, streaming culture provides corporations with the opportunity to monetize every instance of consumption. Streaming technology enables an economy (i.e. unending consumption) whereby consumers spend more for the same amount of consumptive time.

I laid the book out in a way that readers can pick and choose chapters or read them in their desired order. Chapter 2 provides some theoretical orientation for the book. It explores the way digital retail "disrupted" analog distribution chan-nels. Here the disruption to retail happens from streaming, but also from other forms of digital technology. The chapter begins with a brief history of the point-of-sales (i.e. barcode) system and its application to streaming. Four main concepts are introduced: sharing, disruption, distribution, and disin-termediation. All four terms point toward eliminating the "middle man," but as this chapter shows, intermediaries are entrenched in the cultural content distribution system.

Chapters 3 through 7 highlight specific media forms that now utilize streaming platforms. I begin with music in Chapter 3. Streaming is now the dominant way that people listen to music. This chapter begins by tracing the history of digital distribution from the CD to Napster to iTunes and to Spotify. Propelling the push from one distribution network to the next is a business model called the "album replacement cycle." I discuss the relationship between the album replacement cycle and the constant quest for new ways to distribute music. Then, this chapter explores the way music fans' listening practices changed as a result of streaming. Finally, I look at alternatives to the mainstream streaming services available on the Internet.

Chapter 4 explores the ways that simultaneous release, widescreen television, and made-for-streaming films changed the cultural position of film. Streaming movies makes movies more accessible, which reinvigorates the independent movie scene (i.e. films produced by non-major studios). I discuss how websites such as Vimeo allow amateur filmmakers to distribute their ideas. Finally, this chapter considers how film content has changed because streaming service releases do not have to comply with the MPAA's moving picture board.

Chapter 5 explores the reasons why streaming television is often described as golden age of TV. First, I trace a short history from VHS/Betamax tapes through Reality TV to DVRs. Then I discuss the way streaming services disrupt the political economy of television. A key term explored in this chapter is "flow" – the way television patterns help determine our consumption. Since we are no longer beholden to broadcast schedules, flow is interrupted allowing new cultural forms to develop alongside streaming television. Then I discuss the way streaming services change the political economy of television. In the next section, I discuss binge-watching. One key to how our television culture has changed is the fact that we binge shows like a long movie. Next, I explore how cultural innovations associated with streaming technology developed the golden age of television. Finally, I consider the way streaming television creates new modes of cultural interaction in the conclusion to this chapter.

Video games have been fixed to physical systems and physical software, since their invention. Chapter 6 explores the ways that downloads and streams have changed the design of video games and the cultures that arise along them. First, I explain how the disintermediation of video games changed the content of video games. Here we see dramatic changes in the political economy of video games with a new emphasis on free games supported by advertising and in-game purchases. Second, I discuss the ways that online gaming developed its own cultures from esports to in-game friendships. As gaming platforms (i.e. Nintendo Switch, Microsoft Xbox, etc.) emphasize playing with others online, a parallel service enables the streaming of game play. The chapter concludes by discussing the way gaming platforms invite gamers to participate in broader communities.

In Chapter 7, I introduce the reader to Raymond Williams' theory of emergent culture. Williams lays out three types of culture: Dominant, Residual, and Emergent. This triad of cultural forms provides the structure for the rest of the chapter. First, I discuss briefly the dominant forms as illustrated by Netflix, Spotify, and Amazon. Next, I demonstrate how residual forms remain relevant by discussing vinyl records. Finally, in the bulk of the chapter, I apply this framework to emergent cultural forms: Twitch and Vloggers. Each of these services present new cultural forms that emerged since streaming's development.

In the concluding chapter, I provide an exploration of how we can engage streaming without losing ourselves to the stream, and I discuss potential directions streaming might take in the coming years.

NOTES

1. Henry Jenkins, *Convergence Culture: Where Old and New Media Collide* (New York: New York University Press, 2006), 290.
2. Christian Fuchs, *Social Media: A Critical Introduction* (Thousand Oaks: SAGE, 2013).
3. Rebecca Blood, *We've Got Blog: How Weblogs Are Changing Our Culture* (New York: Basic Books, 2002), ix.

4. Stuart Hall, Jessica Evans, and Sean Nixon, eds., *Representation*, 2nd ed. (London: SAGE; The Open University, 2013).
5. Raymond Williams, "'Culture Is Ordinary' (1958)," in *Resources of Hope: Culture, Democracy, Socialism* (Verso Books, 1989), 3-14.
6. Paul du Gay et al., *Doing Cultural Studies: The Story of the Sony Walkman*, 2nd ed. (Los Angeles: SAGE, 2013); Hall, Evans, and Nixon, *Representation*.
7. Stuart Hall, "Encoding, Decoding," in *The Cultural Studies Reader*, ed. Simon During, 3rd vol. (London; New York: Routledge, 2007), xii, 564 p., http://www.loc.gov/catdir/toc/fy0906/2009286081.html.
8. Hall.
9. Steven Levitan and Christopher Lloyd, *Modern Family* (Levitan/Lloyd, 20th Century Fox Television, Steven Levitan Productions, 2009), television.
10. Alex Moaba, "Ann Romney Likes 'Modern Family,' But Show's Creator Pushes Back," *HuffPost*, August 28, 2012, Online edition, sec. TV & Film, https://www.huffpost.com/entry/modern-family-ann-romney_n_1837171.
11. Vincent Mosco, *Becoming Digital: Toward a Post-Internet Society* (Bingley: Emerald Publishing Limited, 2017).
12. Timm Böttger et al., "Open Connect Everywhere: A Glimpse at the Internet Ecosystem through the Lens of the Netflix CDN," *ArXiv:1606.05519 [Cs]*, June 17, 2016, http://arxiv.org/abs/1606.05519.
13. Nick Srnicek, *Platform Capitalism* (Cambridge; Malden: Polity, 2017), 23.
14. Max Horkheimer and Theodor W. Adorno, "The Culture Industry: Enlightenment as Mass Deception," in *Dialectic of Enlightenment* (New York: Herder and Herder, 1972), xvii, 258 p.
15. Patrick Burkart and Tom McCourt, *Digital Music Wars: Ownership and Control of the Celestial Jukebox* (New York: Rowman & Littlefield Publishers, 2006).
16. Stanley Cohen, *Folk Devils and Moral Panics: The Creation of the Mods and Rockers* (New York: Routledge, 2011), http://public.eblib.com/EBLPublic/PublicView.do?ptiID=684015; David Arditi, "Downloading Is Killing Music: The Recording Industry's Piracy Panic Narrative," ed. Victor Sarafian and Rosemary Findley, *Civilisations*, The

State of the Music Industry, 63, no. 1 (July 2014): 13-32; William Patry, *Moral Panics and the Copyright Wars* (New York: Oxford University Press, 2009).

17. David Arditi, *ITake-Over: The Recording Industry in the Streaming Era*, 2nd ed. (Lanham: Lexington Books, 2020).

18. Lynn Spigel, *Welcome to the Dreamhouse: Popular Media and Postwar Suburbs* (Durham: Duke University Press Books, 2001).

19. Chuck Tryon, *On-Demand Culture: Digital Delivery and the Future of Movies*, None edition (New Brunswick: Rutgers University Press, 2013), 4.

20. Horkheimer and Adorno, "The Culture Industry: Enlightenment as Mass Deception."

21. David Arditi, "Digital Subscriptions: The Unending Consumption of Music in the Digital Era," *Popular Music and Society* 41, no. 3 (2018): 302-18, https://doi.org/10.1080/03007766.2016.1264101.

22. Michel Aglietta, *A Theory of Capitalist Regulation: The US Experience*, trans. David Fernbach, New edition (New York: Verso, 2001); Paul Smith, *Millennial Dreams: Contemporary Culture and Capital in the North*, The Haymarket Series (London; New York: Verso, 1997).

23. Ben Agger, *Fast Capitalism* (Urbana: University of Illinois Press, 1988).

24. Ben Agger, *Speeding Up Fast Capitalism: Cultures, Jobs, Families, Schools, Bodies* (Boulder: Routledge, 2004).

25. Mosco, *Becoming Digital.*

26. Agger, *Speeding Up Fast Capitalism.*

27. Jodi Dean, *Blog Theory: Feedback and Capture in the Circuits of Drive*, 1st ed. (Malden, MA: Polity, 2013), 2-3.

28. Arditi, "Digital Subscriptions."

2

DIGITAL RETAIL: DISRUPTION, DISTRIBUTION, AND DISINTERMEDIATION

An infamous video shows former President George H.W. Bush next to a shopping clerk scanning a carton of orange juice. The 1992 campaign video shows Bush struggling to get the orange juice to scan. The video led to the feeling that Bush Sr. was out of touch with the American people.[1] While some people dispute the scanner amazed Bush Sr., the message was clear: barcodes were part of everyday life. Today, we wrestle with barcodes in the self-checkout lines at grocery stores everywhere. Airports move our luggage using barcodes. Packages delivered by UPS, USPS, and FedEx utilize barcodes to track their delivery, etc. However, the importance of the barcode lies not in its ubiquity, but its capacity to foster change in the retail chain.

The Universal Product Code (UPC) first developed in the 1970s as a means to speed-up the checkout process at grocery stores. Deploying the UPC was one step in the long march of self-service that places more labor on the consumer.[2]

UPCs enabled what is now known as point-of-sale systems, communication networks that utilize barcodes to register a sale and store data about the transaction. When someone purchases a good at a store, the retailer transmits data about the sale to the producer. Barcode provides an early deployment of what we now call "big data." Big data is a euphemism that refers to surveillance of our digital behavior deployed across multiple networks from search requests to credit card sales and driving apps to loyalty card tags. These technologies enable the smooth functioning of capital while turning everything into a data point. The process is not new, but continues to change the way we interact with culture.

In 1991, the year before Bush Sr.'s trip to the grocery store, *Billboard* magazine changed the way that it measured music sales for its music charts. The old system involved surveying record store clerks about perceived sales. This made the system rife for tampering. Record labels knew which stores would be surveyed and would give clerks swag (t-shirts, concert tickets, etc.) for fudging the numbers. *Billboard* was aware of how dubious the system was, but it worked better than relying on recording industry data—labels reported "shipments" not sales, and shipment data do not include numbers about what was shipped back to labels. As a result, *Billboard* fundamentally changed its media measurement by incorporating Nielsen SoundScan. The new measurement system utilized UPC barcodes to count sales at the point-of-sale. This gave real-time data to Nielsen, *Billboard*, and major record labels. They immediately noticed discrepancies between what they thought sold and what actually sold.[3] Labels and *Billboard* discovered that hip-hop and country music outperformed what they imagined. They also realized that the primary consumers of hip-hop music were white suburban teenage boys—the music produced changed accordingly. The barcode changed the music retail system.

Perhaps more significantly, barcodes and point of sale altered the retail clothing industry. Retail stores purchase clothing on a global market without knowing what will sell from style to size. With the acceleration of globalization, production moves from the rich global north countries to the poor global south countries.[4] However, manufacturing massive amounts of clothing across the world takes time to get from production to retail. The result was oversupply of most fashions and the rise of outlet stores. Point-of-sale systems reduced overproduction by creating what is now known as "just in time" production. A retail outlet registers a sale using barcodes, which gets reported to the company providing real-time reports on what is in stock. If a style or size sells quickly, clothing companies can tap into communication systems to order more of a specific style or size and have them delivered in shortened time.

Streaming has similar results. In the television world, producers and streaming platforms receive real-time data about consumption on everything from the content of the shows to the demographics of the viewers. This changes what television is produced. In music, labels recognize that a viral TikTok star has the power to drive consumption in the moment even if no one remembers them in a year. They sign these acts knowing they can generate a hefty profit. In film, producers can experiment with low-budget films "made for streaming" because it allows studios to see what content is trending.

Part of the enthusiasm for digital retail distribution stems from cutting out the intermediary—also known as disintermediation. By dealing directly with consumers, retailers argue, on the one hand, this "disrupts" traditional networks. On the other hand, they celebrate this as a massive change that brings "freedom."

Changes in the retail system trend toward greater effi-
ciency, while internet celebrants declare these changes amount
to disruption. Here I demonstrate contrary to theories of
disruption, new technologies provide oil to the machine that is
capitalism.

SHARING

Probably the greatest internet-related euphemism is "sharing."
When we access the World Wide Web, we provide bits of
information about ourselves to the world. These bits of information could be music files on our computers, they could be
what we ate for lunch, or they could be demographic data
about us. However, the ubiquity of sharing in digital networks
reframes how we think about splitting something so others
can enjoy the thing too. We all know what happens when a
child is confronted by having another child in their play space.
Child A wants to play with a toy, but Child B has possession
of the toy. If the toy is Child A's, their guardian will implore
them to "share." If someone has a slice of chocolate cake and
another person's mouth begins salivating for the cake, the
cake owner may decide to split the cake in half to "share" it.
We're taught that sharing is a selfless act to make others
feel better and increase social goodwill. However, internet
parlance aims to enjoy increased social goodwill, while leaving
actual users estranged from their friends and their data.

There is reason to celebrate the sharing potential of the
Internet. Because we can email or send whatever files we want
to other people, sharing is a valuable concept in the streaming
era. We get the first glimpses of the power of "sharing" with
Napster—the first digital file-sharing website. But digital
sharing began earlier. For instance, AOL Instant Messenger

provided the first mechanism I could use to send files directly to friends. Other internet users cite Internet Relay Chat (IRC), message boards, or personal websites as the first mechanism to share information. Of course, there has always been a limitation on one's ability to share files because whether you try to send files via email or messaging services, they often limit the size of files. Even today, Google requires users to upload larger files to Google Drive instead of attaching them to emails in Gmail. Napster fixed the problem of sharing larger files, but content industries viewed file-sharing websites as cesspools of piracy. Content owners mobilized this rhetoric to maintain control over cultural content and the profit it generates.

Enter the beauty of YouTube. By uploading files to this central service and making them available to all, users can upload videos and send links to friends. Then users can stream videos at their convenience. However, YouTube is an intermediary that can provide a check on videos to make sure users have permission to upload the videos and is a source of censorship. "YouTube is not actually in the video business – its business, rather, is the provision of a convenient and usable platform for online video *sharing*: users (some of them premium content partners) supply the content, which in turn brings new participants and new audiences."[5] While the emphasis is on the sharing of online video content, this conception of sharing is not devoid of the implications of sharing presented in the euphemistic notions of sharing— i.e., exploitation. When users utilize YouTube to distribute videos, whether self-created or not, they provide the content creation for Google. At times this service is curatorial, but the most important part is the videos users create themselves. YouTube users share information about themselves, Google collects data on users, and Google sells data to third parties. While users share information about themselves with other users, at the same time, they provide a source of endless revenue for the platform.

I identify three types of sharing on the Internet: (1) providing something to someone else (ex. file-sharing), (2) disclosing information about oneself (ex. Facebook status update), and (3) companies selling user information with other companies. All three types of sharing obscure power dynamics on the Internet through the language of sharing. As internet culture transitions to streaming culture, the fundamental dynamic for sharing in a streaming economy relies on the third sense of the term—i.e. selling user information.

First, sharing became popular on digital networks with the rise of peer-to-peer file-sharing services. The initial enthusiasm and fear about sharing stemmed from the popularity of Napster, and later, Kazaa, Grokster, Gnutella, LimeWire, and BitTorrent. However, sharing files on digital networks began with the first email sent in 1971. This exchange of bits and bytes was an exchange of information. The difference between a text-based email and an email containing a music or movie file differs only in the number of 1s and 0s (binary code) the exchange transfers. The first instance I can remember of being able to transfer files directly to friends happened over AOL Instant Messenger (AIM). These direct chat conversations through AIM facilitated instant communication over digital networks. More advanced internet users used internet relay chat (IRC) and message boards to transfer information over the Internet. The primary difference between file-sharing services and other means to exchange information is in the file-sharing platforms' own descriptive emphasis on exchanging files. At the time they developed, file-sharing platforms facilitated a more efficient way of sharing information with others than email, instant messaging, and message boards. Furthermore, they enabled users to find files on other people's computers—often people they didn't know. This is the closest form of sharing to a dictionary definition because it allows someone to split, copy, and give files to others.

Second, sharing means "to tell" other people about things happening in your life.[6] Social networking websites are infamous for allowing people to tell others about every mundane detail of their lives. From food pictures on Instagram to public descriptions of break-ups, we can tell others about everything that happens to us—whether they want to know about it or not. In this sense of the word, we "overshare." As Ben Agger describes in *Oversharing*, "Sharing used to mean splitting your dessert with your significant other. Now, it means spilling your guts, going public with intimate details of your life. Oversharing is telling too much."[7] We publicly post things we wouldn't otherwise dream of letting strangers know about us. While this shared information is usually mundane, our compulsion to share our thoughts and actions creates a comfort with sending intimate details about our lives. I'm not the sharing police, and I'm certainly guilty of oversharing, but the moment represents a change in culture. We voluntarily provide intimate details about our lives to strangers and acquaintances—people who otherwise have no idea about our daily lives. Social media platforms specialize in providing us space to share our lives with others. Facebook asks us to post "What's on your mind?" and we can "share" others' posts. Twitter asks, "What's happening?" Instagram invites us to share "Your Story." But why do Facebook, Twitter, and Instagram want us to provide information? Our sharing is their business—by this I mean, social media companies profit from us telling others our intimate life details.

Third, sharing means selling. This is the dark underbelly of the first two meanings of sharing. As we share information with others, the platforms we use collect data about us. In the user agreements and privacy policies of every online platform from social media to movie theater apps, we permit these platforms to "share" our data with "third parties"—third parties can be anything from companies to police. In some cases, such as the agreement between Amazon's Ring Doorbell and local police departments, companies provide the information free of charge to law enforcement agencies. But in the more usual sense of the term, the privacy policy provisions that state they "share" information with third parties means that they sell the data. For example, in Facebook's 2012 privacy policy the "words sharing/share appear 85 times. . . the terms sell/selling/sale not a single time."[8] Our data is their commodity. Several theories exist about whether we are the commodity, the data is the commodity, we are workers for the companies, or we are fairly compensated for our data.[9] In every case, online platforms sell our data with permission through our user agreements. These policies sometimes give the option to opt-out, but the process is usually laborious. Most people click accept on the privacy policy or terms of use with little thought about what they give platforms in return. Furthermore, while most of us don't bat an eyelash at a private company sharing our data for profit, many more people demonstrate concern when it's the government.[10] Surveillance of our internet activity creates data that companies exploit for profit.

Through the rhetoric of internet proponents, sharing, a distinctly non-capitalist cultural practice, morphs into a decidedly capitalist enterprise. This is one instance where digital networks foster unending consumption. Streams of data become commodified by platforms through surveillance systems. Streaming services increase the number and types of data sources available for technology corporations. For instance, as we watch television shows on Netflix, we provide demographic data, temporal information about how long we watch a certain show and how quickly we watch a season, data about other shows we watch, and if we login with Facebook, we provide all sorts of information about us and our friends. These data allow Netflix to better market to us, produce shows they think we want, and of course, provide data the company can then "share" with (i.e. sell to) third parties. At the same time, internet celebrants tell us the Internet disrupts our culture, social norms, and business practices.

DISRUPTION

As early as 1995,[11] internet prognosticators predicted that the Internet would disrupt the world as we know it. Disruption is a dominant theme in internet discourse. In 1999, the music industry claimed disruption caused by Napster would kill recorded music. In the early 2000s, the dot-com bubble promised to replace old businesses with new. Internet utopians believed the Internet would bring democracy to everyone around the world in the 1990s and social media utopians believed the same thing in 2011. How has the Internet disrupted society? The answer: the dominant change the Internet fosters is a change to business models while we still long for democratic change.

Look at Amazon. In 1994, Jeff Bezos founded Amazon (then Cadabra) as a means to sell books online. This was a watershed moment in the history of retail, unbeknownst to anyone at the time. But we also see a cascading effect that repeats itself throughout the retail industry regardless of product. In the 1990s, big corporate book chains put small independent bookstores out of business. The big corporate bookstores of Barnes and Noble, Books-A-Million, and Borders provided large retail outlets for books, calendars, and stationary with an emphasis on a very specific market: best-selling books. They place the best-sellers in center aisles and the other rows of books are known in the industry as "wall-paper" because they create an ambiance, not sales.[12] The result was lower-priced books with less diversity. Independent bookstores always provided a variety of books and still sold best-sellers to stay open. The big corporate bookstores put most small shops out of business. Then Amazon came around and put many big corporate bookstores out of business. Amazon offered an essentially unlimited catalog of books available at the click of a button and delivered to your front door. In the world of academic bookstores, this meant cheaper books available to broke students. Eventually, Amazon launched the Kindle and Barnes and Noble launched the Nook, electronic readers that allow users to read digital books. These electronic devices eliminated the need for physical copies of books. At the same time, Amazon enabled the phenomenon of self-publishing books at a very low cost. Small mom-and-pop bookstores offered space to local authors to sell books on their shelves, but corporate bookstores more-or-less put an end to this practice. In a strange turn, Amazon re-creates the capacity for authors to self-publish.

Amazon has gone on to "disrupt" numerous industries, especially of the cultural variety. But Amazon has created more problems for retail than anything else. Big box retailers from Best Buy to Walmart have the most to lose from Amazon's economic takeover. The bookselling giant turned ubiquitous retail deliverer upended the economy of scale of other predatory retailers.

In this sense "disruption" deals with changes to business practices, not changes to fundamental aspects of society. This disruption represents a shift towards more monopolization than a shift away from it. To disrupt is to interrupt in a way that alters or destroys a process or activity. Disruption in a factory happens when workers go on strike. Disruption to an election occurs when people can't go vote. A hurricane can disrupt education if schools have to close for a period of time due to the storm or its effects. Earthquakes can disrupt roads by cracking them and making them impassable. Pandemics can disrupt everything. For me, disruption can be revolutionary when it overthrows the status quo. When internet prognosticators predicted the Internet would bring democracy, they predicted disruption. This again happened when social media utopians believed that Twitter and Facebook gave us the Arab Spring and Occupy Wall Street. However, neither the Internet nor social media disrupted the dominant order—people showing up to protests changed the status quo. In hindsight, we see in 2020 that we still do not have democracy, and digital networks provide hackers the capacity to disrupt digital voting machines. Additionally, following the 2016 American elections, Brexit Referendum, and other elections, it is clear social media provide platforms for undemocratic disruption as they allow foreign powers to tamper with elections. In any case, the status quo of capitalism and non-democracy continue unabated. The Internet did not disrupt anything, but rather, it changed the way businesses function so they can make higher profits.

DISTRIBUTION AND DISINTERMEDIATION

When we think about how streaming platforms change our cultural landscape, it is important to consider how power plays a role in these transformations. "YouTube clearly represents a disruption to existing media business models and is emerging as a new site of media power."[13] Jean Burgess and Joshua Green sum up the contradictions contained within the rhetoric about digital disruptions. YouTube created "disruption" for the Culture Industry at the same time that it gave corporations more power in the media system. Users create videos and share them with others, but YouTube uses data about users to better market to them thereby increasing Google's profits. Google doesn't care what types of videos you share because as long as users comply with the law, they will distribute any video from ones that criticize Google's work environment to ones that promote other streaming platforms. Digital technology changed the way we receive cultural content. The same processes whereby one technology or business model replaces an old technology or business model take shape on the Internet by eliminating layers of intermediaries accustomed to exploiting new technologies for profit.

In 2020, digital media is first-and-foremost a means to distribute content for profit. Internet utopians of the 1990s imagined the Internet as a platform on which "information wants to be free." However, the influx of venture capital at the turn of the century, which resulted in the dot-com bubble, demonstrated information is profitable. Specifically, information is profitable because it eliminates layers of distribution. Take the newspaper industry, for example. In order to deliver papers, newspapers require printing presses in warehouses with staffs. Then the papers need to go out to readers through a network of deliverers who need to traverse every street in a given geographic area every morning. With a newspaper subscription, each newspaper is relatively cheap for readers as it is subsidized by advertisements. If we look further into the cultural realm at something like film or music, the distribution costs increase. While new costs exist in terms of data storage and digital workers, the Internet has allowed the cost of media distribution to go down and profits to go up.

The driving force behind the profitability of information on the Internet is the process of disintermediation, a big word for a simple concept. Disintermediation means to eliminate things that come between. This all derives from the use of the word media. A medium is something that comes between two things. The plural of medium is media. To intermediate means to come between two things. When we discuss media, we're really discussing communications technology that comes between. Disintermediation specifically means the elimination of intermediaries in the media distribution chain. Intermediaries are colloquially called "middlemen" (despite the patriarchal connotation of the word). When Apple opened iTunes, it eliminated the need for factories that produce compact discs, trucks to distribute the product, warehouses to store CDs, and physical retailers. This is disintermediation at work.

Furthermore, disintermediation refers to the blurring of text and video. "The general digitization of channels and information erases the differences among individual media. Sound and image, voice and text are reduced to surface effects, known to consumers as interface."[14] Here YouTube provides the quintessential example. YouTube is a video streaming platform, but it is also the most popular platform to listen to music. Major record labels dislike the dominance of YouTube as a medium to listen to music because video consumption offers less money back to labels under existing copyright legislation.[15] The blurring of video and music is at the heart of disintermediation in streaming culture.

What cannot be lost in the process of disintermediation is the decreasing costs to Culture Industry producers as a result of the elimination of intermediaries. If we just think about the cost of a CD, the CD must be manufactured and printed, the packaging must be created, CDs must be stored before sale, at each stage the various parts must be shipped from various warehouses to other warehouses, CDs are distributed to retailers, and retailers mark-up the price approximately $6 on their end. All of these costs are more or less eliminated when internet distribution disintermediates music. While the transition from CD or DVD to download transformed the cultural commodity through disintermediation, the form remained resolutely in the same realm of commodity. Instead of buying CDs, disintermediation allowed music listeners to buy computer files. These computer files allowed content producers to "wire shut"[16] the uses of the files by only permitting certain uses, but the cultural consumption still emphasized buying and collecting. The shift from down-loading to streaming further solidified a transition from owning to renting. Hence the need to think in terms of unending consumption.

Streaming not only disintermediates, it de-acquisitions because we no longer own, but rather perpetually subscribe. The goal of producers shifts from producing new cultural content for people to purchase to providing access to new and old content. The new content sweetens the pot to entice sub-scribers to stay subscribed, but the economics of cultural consumption shift. People subscribe for immediate access to get their fix of cultural content, but it ensures that few cultural artifacts stay popular for long. "Capitalism in the contem-porary era needs to find ways to liquidate inventory, keeping people in the malls and showrooms so that their shopping transforms inventory into profit."[17] As with fast capitalism, unending consumption happens at a time when cultural pro-ducers create large quantities of cultural content, but in the content's ubiquity, few people listen to, read, watch, play or use the bulk of this content. The logic of subscription services is not to have people listen to, read, watch, play or use any specific content closely, but rather to entice them to subscribe. Since subscribers can never consume all of the content, they stay subscribed to try to reach the end. In 2002, following an early meme, DirecTV DSL created a commercial where a guy reaches the "end of the Internet."[18] With Spotify, Netflix, Amazon, and YouTube, it is impossible to reach the end of their libraries, so subscribers remain on the hook. As political theorist Jodi Dean describes "communicative capitalism," the turbulence of networks creates "the rapidity of innovation, adoption, adaptation, and obsolescence."[19] Subscriptions intervene in this process by allowing subscribers to ignore the obsolescence of cultural content and perpetually access the new. Distribution ceases to limit access, but the question becomes access to what?

As I mentioned above, Amazon created the circumstances where authors can easily self-publish their work, but to what end? It turns out that the disintermediation afforded by digital networks also exponentially increases the volume of self-published work. Now, anyone can publish a book, but this makes it even more difficult to earn a living writing books. Fast capitalism marks a moment when the world publishes many books, but no one has time to read them. If everyone becomes a self-published author on Amazon, a few people may sell a decent number of books, while most people may sell a copy or two. Selling one copy of a book does not net much revenue for any individual, but Amazon earns revenue from every sale through its store. The same logic undergirds Spotify. For 1,000 plays, an artist earns roughly $7.50, not enough to buy lunch nonetheless pay rent, but Spotify brings in $9.99/ month per subscription regardless of who a subscriber listens to or how much they listen to music. The volume of content available through streaming platforms enables the platform companies and large corporate cultural producers to generate massive amounts of revenue while the creators themselves earn pennies.

The disintermediation of the cultural distribution system does not create disruption; it drives profit. Thinking about streaming platforms as digital distributors helps to reevaluate how streaming culture interfaces with the economy.

Disintermediation does not end distribution, it just makes it more profitable for large corporations.

CONCLUSION

Distribution changes retail, but it does not disrupt it. Video rental stores, music stores, and video game stores closed during the digital transition, but the commodity logic for cultural goods remains as strong as ever. For instance, while we may no longer have the option to visit physical retailers like Blockbuster, an economy of movie rentals persists. Now we stream our weekend movies from Amazon, Disney+, Netflix, or Hulu. These services license films from movie studios, but retailers no longer have to pay rent, electricity, or clerks. Disruption in distribution parallels new (more efficient) sources of revenue for content producers.

To discuss streaming culture is to discuss retail. Since streaming changed how we access culture, it transformed the political economy of the retail business. Whether we think about Amazon trucks delivering things to our door or Netflix movies streaming on our smart TVs, digital networks and later streaming services led disintermediating processes. But I do not think the term disruption has the correct connotations to address this shift. Film and TV studios, record labels, and video game producers consider these shifts when they produce content, but they did not disrupt anything. Rather, cultural content producers embrace these changes to inhibit greater profits. Creating disintermediated distribution networks fosters unending consumption. Now instead of buying something once and devoting one's attention to other cultural items, we are fixated on the new. This fixation keeps us subscribing and sharing our data with corporations.

NOTES

1. Andrew Rosenthal, "Bush Encounters the Supermarket, Amazed," *The New York Times*, February 5, 1992, sec. U.S., https://www.nytimes.com/1992/02/05/us/bush-encounters-the-supermarket-amazed.html.
2. Michael Palm, *Technologies of Consumer Labor: A History of Self-Service* (New York: Routledge, 2016).
3. S. Craig Watkins, *Hip Hop Matters: Politics, Pop Culture, and the Struggle for the Soul of a Movement* (Boston: Beacon Press, 2005).
4. Paul Smith, "Tommy Hilfiger in the Age of Mass Customization," in *No Sweat: Fashion, Free Trade, and the Rights of Garment Workers*, ed. Andrew Ross (London: Verso, 1997).
5. Jean Burgess et al., *YouTube: Online Video and Participatory Culture*, 1st ed. (Cambridge; Malden: Polity, 2009), 4.
6. Ben Agger, *Oversharing: Presentations of Self in the Internet Age* (New York: Routledge, 2011), 44.
7. Agger, 3.
8. Christian Fuchs, *Social Media: A Critical Introduction* (Thousand Oaks: SAGE Publications Ltd, 2013), 166.
9. Fuchs, *Social Media*.
10. Brian Connor and Long Doan, "Government vs. Corporate Surveillance: Privacy Concerns in the Digital World," in *The Dialectic of Digital Culture*, ed. David Arditi and Jennifer Miller (Lanham: Rowman & Littlefield, 2019), 47–60.
11. Joseph L. Bower and Clayton M. Christensen, "Disruptive Technologies: Catching the Wave," *Harvard Business Review*, January 1, 1995, https://hbr.org/1995/01/disruptive-technologies-catching-the-wave.
12. David Grazian, *Mix It Up: Popular Culture, Mass Media, and Society*, 2nd ed. (New York: W.W. Norton, Incorporated, 2017), 197.
13. Burgess et al., *YouTube*, 15.
14. Friedrich A. Kittler, *Gramophone, Film, Typewriter* (Stanford, CA: Stanford University Press, 1999), 1.
15. David Arditi, "Digital Hegemony: Net Neutrality, the Value Gap, and Corporate Interests," in *The Dialectic of Digital Culture*, ed. David Arditi and Jennifer Miller (Lanham: Lexington Books, 2019), 13-28.

16. Tarleton Gillespie, *Wired Shut: Copyright and the Shape of Digital Culture* (Cambridge: MIT Press, 2007).
17. Ben Agger, *Speeding Up Fast Capitalism: Cultures, Jobs, Families, Schools, Bodies* (Boulder: Routledge, 2004), 16.
18. *2002 DirecTV DSL "End of the Internet" Commercial*, accessed March 5, 2020, https://www.youtube.com/watch?v=_uXtWIg_A7M.
19. Jodi Dean, *Blog Theory: Feedback and Capture in the Circuits of Drive*, 1st ed. (Cambridge: Polity, 2013), 1.

3

STREAMING MUSIC: UNENDING CONSUMPTION BEGINS

When I was a junior in high school, Napster launched. I remember the day my friend messaged me through AOL Instant Messenger to tell me about the new file-sharing service where we could find all kinds of music. After downloading the software, I searched "Dave Matthews Band" and found dozens of live shows in addition to the band's studio albums. At the time, this was a big deal for a number of reasons. First, there was no great website to collect music. Mp3.com allowed users to download music, but options were limited to independent musicians who owned the copyrights to their music. Second, download speeds were notoriously slow and listening to music online was more painful than early Sony Discmans on a bumpy road (note: they didn't have skip protection and skipped repeatedly). Third, finding bootlegs of Dave Matthews Band shows was next to impossible. You needed to know someone who knew someone who recorded the shows. As a high schooler it was far more difficult to be in the know than for college-aged people.

Napster changed all of this, but at the time, few people would know what music consumption would look like in 20 years. This chapter begins by tracing the history of digital distribution from the CD to Napster to iTunes to streaming services. Propelling the push from one distribution network to the next is a business model called the "album replacement cycle." Next, I argue that Apple's purchase of Beats Music marked the moment music left the download era and entered the streaming era. Then, I explore the way music fans' listening practices changed as a result of streaming. Here an emphasis of the chapter is on the use of both playlists and algorithmic song selection. Finally, I look at alternatives to the mainstream streaming services available on the Internet. While celebrants of the Internet have celebrated the potential for alternatives to the mainstream, most services have not lived up to these expectations and the major labels still dominate music production.

THE ALBUM REPLACEMENT CYCLE

In many respects, streaming music was the next logical step for music consumption. The music industry has always worked on the logic of selling content (software) to be played on music hardware. Not long after Thomas Edison and Emile Berliner invented the phonograph and gramophone (respectively), gramophone manufacturers discovered the better way to make profits came from selling content for the machines instead of selling the machines themselves. At the time, gramophones were novelties, and no one wanted more than one per home. In fact, listening to music alone in a room was seen as taboo. Gramophone manufacturers didn't even know what people would want to listen to. The iconic logo of a dog looking into a gramophone for RCA Records began as an ad-campaign by the record label's predecessor, the Victor Talking Machine Co. In the original ad-campaign from the late 19th century, the accompanying text read "His Master's Voice" – the idea being that gramophones could record people's voices the same way photographs retained their image, then we could hear our relatives' voices long after they passed away. Gramophone records were also a way to release speeches in an era before television, film and mass radio broadcasts—imagine being able to listen to President Abraham Lincoln's "Gettysburg Address."

Eventually, gramophone manufacturers realized people wanted to purchase music to play on their gramophones and there was more money to be made through selling musical recordings than selling gramophones. This is known as the expansion of the means of consumption,[1] a practice nearly universally adopted by various arms of the Culture Industry. Basically, once a market becomes saturated for hardware like gramophones, capitalists can continue to generate revenue by producing commodities to be played on the hardware. Additionally, the music industry deploys planned obsolescence as a means to expand consumption further. The planned obsolescence of cultural goods stems from music, film, television, etc. becoming outdated or boring to use over time. People listen to a record for a while, they get bored with it, and they want new music, so record labels produce new music for people to listen to, and more importantly, to buy.

However, even the purchasing of new music has its limits. If someone buys a record of their favorite artist, they can listen to it indefinitely without ever paying to hear it again. Probably my most listened to album is a CD copy of the Red Hot Chili Peppers' *Blood, Sugar, Sex, Magik,* which my sister gave to me around 1995. My sister got bored with

it and gave it to me, but I have never tired of the Chili
Peppers' funkiest album. For folks who obsessively listen to
the same album repeatedly, cultural planned obsolescence
must be met with technological obsolescence. If you can't
play your favorite album on your newest device, you have
to purchase the album in a *new* format. When the recording
industry can't get consumers to buy new music, they make
them buy the music they already own to play it on a new
technology.

The album replacement cycle is the process through which
people repurchase music they own on new media. For
instance, someone may own an album on vinyl (33 1/3-rpm),
but then purchase it on CD to be able to listen to it on their
CD player. As a process of the expansion of the means of
consumption, the album replacement cycle ensures record
labels' periodic growth from catalog recordings—recordings
that have been on the market at least 18 months. There is no
functional way to play 33 1/3 record on a CD player, so
people repurchase their music. Keep in mind taping a vinyl
record on a tape cassette has been upheld in the United States
as a form of fair use. However, record labels attempt to
incentivize the album replacement cycle and deter home
recording/copying. In the 1980s, the British Phonographic
Industry (the British trade association for record labels)
proffered an ad campaign with the slogan "Home Taping is
Killing Music" with the express goal of deterring music listeners from taping their vinyl records.[2] Each new music
format drives steep growth in the recording industry as
demand increases for catalog recordings whereas demand for
new releases remains relatively consistent.

Four elements have driven changes to technology in the
album replacement cycle: capacity, fidelity, portability and
convenience. At times these elements moved together, but
sometimes a gain for one element meant a decline for another

element. With each new technology, music fans needed to replace their albums in the new format. First, new recording technologies often provided larger storage capacity. The original gramophone records only held about 3 minutes of music per side of the disc. This led social theorist Theodor Adorno to exhort "the only thing that can characterize gramophone music is the inevitable brevity dictated by the size of the shellac plate."[3] The brevity dictated by the technological form has had an outsized impact on the length of popular songs, which still average about 3 minutes in length. Now that digital music files and streaming cloud services provide limitless capacity, songs continue to adhere to the 3-minute length. The transition from 78-rpm record to the 33 1/3 record created changes that reverberated through the industry as songs stretched longer and the idea of an album as a collection of songs developed. Along with the collection of songs afforded by these longer records, many musicians began recording "concept albums"—a collection of songs that followed an overall theme.

Second, new technologies tend to provide higher fidelity. Early 78-rpm records consistently improved in fidelity over the years, partly driven by better recording processes. However, the release of the longer 33 1/3 records also marked a significant improvement in sound fidelity. This watershed moment was the first time a new technology drove music listeners to purchase their music anew. Yet the bigger moment for sound fidelity came in 1958 with the wide release of stereo records. Stereo sound drove people to purchase new "stereos" (the ubiquitous term we use to describe any music player that include speakers). With stereos in their homes, music fans needed their old music in the new format and labels worked hard to "remaster" old recordings to make them stereo. Of course, every new technology did not include improvements in fidelity. Tape cassettes had lower sound fidelity than vinyl;

mp3s used compression techniques that deteriorated sound fidelity.[4]

Third, portability became a selling point for new technologies following the development of magnetic tape. The first commercially available music playback systems to use magnetic tape were 8-track players. While there were attempts to make vinyl record players for cars, none of these models caught-on. If people wanted to listen to music in their car, they had to listen to radio. This all changed with the 8-track player, which allowed portable music listening. 8-track tapes were far more compact and could hold the same amount of music as a 33 1/3 record. People began installing these machines in their cars. Next came the even more compact and portable tape cassette. Eventually, Sony developed the Sony Walkman, which Sony marketed as a freeing device that allowed people to listen to music through headphones throughout their daily lives.[5] While these machines facilitated the home recording of vinyl records, a surge in catalog sales followed the release of the 8-track and tape cassette players.

Finally, convenience became a new issue as digital music became available online. At the high-point of CDs, you could often get into someone's car and they would have several binders filled with CDs. This was the bulky way people traveled with their music collections. However, traveling with several hundred CDs in your car made them easy targets for thieves—who could then sell the CDs to record stores as used merchandise under the first-sale doctrine in the US. During the tape cassette era, storing tapes in a hot car often resulted in melted tapes. The convenience of traveling with one's music collection was met with the finite existence of a music collection. With both the tape cassette and the CD, record labels benefited from the possible destruction or theft of someone's music collection as they would then have to repurchase the music once again.

Streaming music advances all four elements described here. First, streaming creates limitless capacity because one needs very little space on a playback device to access music in the cloud. Second, streaming creates the capability of higher fidelity. As I write, the major music streaming platforms are developing tiered subscriptions where subscribers can pay more per month for higher fidelity music. There is little technological barrier to providing higher fidelity streams, but with the rise of mp3, many listeners became accustomed to lower fidelity music. Third, since most streamers use their phones to stream music, they have access to their music virtually anywhere. Fourth, streaming music gives users access to a nearly limitless music catalog. As long as an artist has their music on a platform, then it is available. Music listeners don't have to worry about having their CDs stolen or their tapes melted. At the same time streaming achieves each of these four elements, streaming music brings the album replacement cycle to an end as it institutes unending consumption. Music listeners no longer replace their music collections, but rather, continually pay for access to a service. This new form of the expansion of the means of consumption perpetuates revenue without having to develop new technologies or new music to drive demand.

BEATS, SPOTIFY, APPLE AND THE STREAMING ERA

Apple's decision to purchase Beats in 2014 marked the end of the download era. The $3 billion acquisition of both the popular headphones Beats by Dre and the music streaming service Beats Music proved to be a watershed moment in the music industry. Beats Music was a new service that was quickly growing in size and popularity partly to its new approach to music streaming. As opposed to the à la carte approach of its major rival Spotify, Beats Music used algorithms to direct users to music by activity, taste, and mood. Additionally, Beats hired curators to create playlists—the playlist being a collection of music that mirrored the practice of making mixtapes. When corporations discuss business decisions, they reify the market—i.e., they give it a life beyond reality. Corporations, businesspersons, and economic claims the "market does" something, but in reality people do something. They say consumers want something. However, this reification simply reflects how people with power think about the world. The market does not work outside the realm of people, and it most certainly does not represent some abstract consumer desire. The case of streaming music, and the album replacement cycle more generally, highlights how remote some sort of consumer demand is from the decisions within a corporation.

At the time Apple purchased Beats, Spotify had long established itself as the dominant streaming service. Yet, even Spotify's goliath position in streaming did not allow it to generate a profit until the end of 2018.[6] Spotify launched in 2006—it took a full 12 years before a ubiquitous brand became profitable! Streaming was growing in 2014, but this was in large part due to the support of the major record labels. In order to gain the licensing to stream music, Spotify gave the major record labels equity in the company—after Spotify went public, the labels cashed in significantly. Major labels also had significant equity in Beats, and following Apple's purchase of Beats, Universal grossed $448 million from their 14% stake in the sale, for instance.[7] These are corporate machinations, not a desire of the people.

Yet, there was a strong draw to streaming services underlying music listeners' move to streaming: (seemingly) free music. Napster provided a service to music listeners that allowed them to exchange files with each other over the

Internet. Keep in mind exchanging music has always been part of music cultures. From swapping vinyl records with friends to exchanging mixtapes, people always wanted to share music with friends. The advent of the cassette tape propelled the cultural exchange of music in the 1980s. These tapes freely passed through dozens of hands as a way to bond socially over music. Blank CDs facilitated the exchange of music in the late-90s, and with mixed CDs listeners received high-fidelity music they could download onto a computer. The US Supreme Court repeatedly ruled this type of exchange is legal under fair use standards and the US Congress codified it into law through the Audio Home Recording Act of 1992.[8] Napster was the cultural production that facilitated the cultural exchange of music. Music fans always wanted free music and peer-to-peer file-sharing provided a mechanism for the exchange. Instead of viewing peer-to-peer file-sharing as an aberration and abomination, we need to think of it as the next step in a cultural process.

Viewed as a movement toward free music, major labels' acceptance of streaming music services was driven by a cultural process of music exchange. Major labels always conceived music as a commodity. This goes back to the initial view gramophone manufactures held that the better source of profit was selling music, not selling gramophones. Record industry desires for profit always conflicted with music listeners' desire for music. Labels bolstered the idea that the only way to listen to music was through the purchase of records. However, people never wanted to purchase or consume records, they wanted to listen to music.

Streaming provided record labels with a mechanism to harmonize music listeners' desires with industry greed. By providing music to listeners free with advertisements, record labels gave music fans their dream while concealing the quest for profit. Of course, ad-supported content is not free, and never has been. As a number of media scholars suggest, watching advertisements turns listeners/watchers into commodities and even workers.[9] Music you do not pay for is not the same thing as free music. Eventually, Spotify and Apple Music (among others) seduced many music listeners into $9.99/month subscriptions—sometimes they entice them with lower-priced student accounts, as well. By providing ad-free music to a seemingly limitless catalog of songs for $10/month, labels and music streaming services found a price music listeners would pay for access. Keep in mind the $120/year subscribers pay is 300% higher than the $45/year the average consumer paid throughout the heyday of the CD and download eras.[10]

This perpetual increase in revenue had record label executives salivating and highlights unending consumption. Once a music fans subscribes for $10/month, they subscribe to a service perpetually. With the purchase of music for $45/year, the purchaser has a material commodity that they possess indefinitely. After spending $120 in a year, the music subscriber has nothing other than the hours spent enjoying music through the service. Since they no longer own music,[11] subscribers must continue to subscribe. The cultural impact has been quick as younger people embraced subscriptions and no longer understand why anyone wouldn't subscribe. For example, in three years, my 120 student Introduction to Popular Culture students went from 3 students embarrassed to admit they subscribe to a music service to 110 proud student subscribers. In a conversation I had with them in 2020, students were incredulous to believe anyone would miss-out on nearly infinite access to music for such a low price.

Apple purchased Beats Music and actively killed the music download. By creating Apple Music, Apple worked with major labels in the hope to recreate the success of the iTunes store in the streaming era. In 2019, Apple closed the iTunes store to further distance its brand from the download era. In turn, the decisions made by large corporations about the distribution of music have changed the way we listen to music as a cultural practice.

LISTENING IN THE STREAMING ERA

Listening to music has never been a solitary activity. As I mentioned above, early in the gramophone era, it was taboo to listen to music in one's room by oneself. Why? Before recorded music, listening to music was inherently social because it required at least one performer and at least one listener. Even after people began listening to gramophones alone, music remained inherently social—people had to perform, record, produce, master, market, distribute and sell the music. At each point where people are involved in music, they influence the music in myriad ways. However, an important social function of recorded music has been the cultural process. From music collectors to tape traders, and DJs to playlist makers, people make symbolic meaning out of music and people with similar music tastes form groups (and vice versa). Alongside the music itself, a number of listening practices developed, but streaming music changes these practices.

High Fidelity, the book-turned-movie-turned Hulu streaming TV series, follows Rob, a record store clerk, and shows record store culture. As a physical commodity, recorded music needed a place to be sold. These stores became cultural phenomena in their own right. As *High Fidelity* portrays, record stores are not only sources of music, but also sites of conversation about music. Record store clerks provide their opinions about music and help to shape customers' musical tastes. If someone sees someone picking up similar music to their own tastes or rocking their favorite band's t-shirt, they can start a conversation and maybe a friendship. In my favorite local record store, Forever Young Records in Grand Prairie, Texas, you can buy t-shirts, old collectibles and other band merch in addition to vinyl, CDs, tape cassettes, 8-tracks, and videos. Iconic record stores such as Amoeba Records in San Francisco, CA have live shows and album signings. Record stores usually have an area dedicated to flyers, which advertise music in the local area. These stores, while a monument to commodity consumption, also provide a source of culture, community, and camaraderie.

In the physical music era, friend groups drove music tastes. When you hung-out with a friend, you listened to their music. New friends meant new musical experiences. For instance, I'll never forget being introduced to The Roots my freshman year in college. While I heard "You Got Me" on the radio before, I never sat and listened to them. Then my friend from across the hall in my dorm told me I needed to hear the whole album, *Things Fall Apart*. He burned a copy of the album for me, and I listened to it that night. Following that experience, I purchased The Roots' catalog and began listening to similar artists. A year later, I would hang-out at a friend's apartment where he would introduce me to underground west coast artists—without that friend, I would have never heard Little Brother, Blackalicious or The Coup because they weren't on the radio or readily available in stores. At other times, I experienced the joys of the mixtape, where friends would give me samplings of their own music tastes.

Algorithms and curators increasingly drive music consumption in the streaming era. People don't experience a broad array of new music, but rather the algorithm assumes your tastes. We see this process begin with Pandora Radio's "music genome" project. Working with a musicologist, Pandora developed a sorting system along 450 musical attributes. As Pandora users listen to music, they like, dislike, and skip tracks. Then, the algorithm attempts to decide which characteristics a user prefers over others. The user experiences a machine that does an excellent job choosing music they want to hear, but the user becomes entrapped in a tube that funnels more and more similar music to them. The problem: while a listener may enjoy the specific musical characteristics chosen for them, they may like other music too. As the algorithm chooses a narrower range of songs, the listener doesn't know what they miss because of these choices. As a result, music consumption has become hyper-personal and its cultural value has declined. Pandora doesn't only ignore culture, but also "treats the cultural mapping of music as distortion."[12] For Pandora, music is part of one's taste without being, in social theorist Pierre Bourdieu's terms, part of one's "habitus"—one's cultural dispositions.[13] This is not to say music isn't meaningful because it is. However, meaning derives from the individual instead of the social group under these circumstances. Without cultural input from those around us, we experience less aesthetic difference.[14] Of course, people will always play music for friends and family as part of the cultural process, I'm not saying we don't do this anymore, but there is a shift. Nor am I claiming there is a cultural loss as a result—cultural changes are neither good nor bad. We are witnessing a shift.

One cultural form that exhibits cultural continuity is sharing playlists. Friends share music via playlists. Some people are the consummate opinion leaders in their friend groups who excel at making deeply informed recommendations to their peers. To do this in 2020, these people spend hours constructing playlists to distribute to their friends. Other people continue to form these playlists for their significant others in a similar practice to the mixtape or CD people would give to their girl/boyfriends. This practice is alive and well, but the algorithms and professionally curated playlists on streaming platforms influence it. These platforms operate under a business model, which foregrounds hits over taste.

The goal of labels is to get the highest number of streams for a song in as little time as possible. Record labels have been criticized for adopting a business model that utilizes a quarterly system like other commodities for decades.[15] The idea behind the quarterly system business model relates to how much revenue a label generates in three months of the year. Investors make decisions on their investments in record labels depending on revenues, profits, and losses in a quarter. However, streaming demands labels to move beyond a quarterly system to the moment. When a label releases a song, they want to see it chart immediately. Labels used to work radio DJs to convince them to play a song, as more DJs played a song, it would see exponential growth on the charts. This took time. On streaming platforms, labels work to get songs on playlists at the moment of release, then they utilize an artist's social media reach to propel the song higher. If the song doesn't hit in the first few weeks, labels move on to other songs and the song will not be included on any playlists. Albums are not important because if an artist puts out ten songs and only two become hits, there are wasted streams on the other eight songs. I've noticed when I speak to my undergraduate students, they rarely know the album a song is from and often cannot name the artist. Again, there is nothing wrong with this phenomenon, but it is a shift.

Take Lil Nas X for instance. His song "Old Town Road" stood at Number 1 on the Billboard Hot 100 for a record-setting 19 weeks. It spent a total of 45 weeks on the Hot 100, but this doesn't come close to the number of weeks in the Hot 100 of other hit songs (Imagine Dragons holds that title for 87 weeks with "Radioactive").[16] As of writing, Lil Nas X has had two other songs chart: "Panini" peaked at Number 5 and stayed on the charts for 32 weeks; "Rodeo" peaked at Number 22 and charted for nine weeks. Lil Nas X's power was the virality of "Old Town Road" supported by his own aptitude to create memes.

USER-GENERATED MUSIC STREAMING PLATFORMS

Internet utopians have propagated the myth that the World Wide Web levels the playing field for independent producers of all types. However, in the music industry, digital distribution has reinforced the power of the major record labels by creating new gatekeepers.[17] The major streaming services do not allow users to upload their music partly because of licensing deals they have with the major labels that prohibit user-generated content. Spotify allowed users to upload content for a brief period, but ultimately shut the system down. However, two user-generated platforms demonstrate the potential and failure of user-generated content: SoundCloud and BandCamp. These "producer-oriented" platforms are "designed in such a way as to encourage producers of music to upload content."[18] Both SoundCloud and BandCamp present opportunities and challenges for musicians hoping to make it in the streaming era. The biggest challenge for both platforms stems from the crowded nature of these platforms, which require musicians to do something to break-through the noise.

While pundits often celebrate SoundCloud as the service that allows musicians to make it in the music business, the celebrations need to be met with skepticism. In one June 2017 New York Times article, journalist Jon Caramanica declared "SoundCloud rap — a swelling subgenre that takes its name from its creators' preferred streaming service — which in the last year has become the most vital and disruptive new movement in hip-hop."[19] This led to "a new ecosystem of rising stars, who ascend quicker than ever — releasing songs that get millions of listens, booking nationwide tours, selling merchandise — without traditional gatekeepers."[20] But does this mean anyone can rise from obscurity to fame like XXXTentacion, Lil Peep, Lil Pump or Lil Uzi Vert? No. More than 20 million musicians have uploaded their music to SoundCloud, but only a handful have found stardom. With millions of musicians uploading music, the question becomes how to break through the noise. These artists excel at using social media to tap into the moment. For instance, Lil Nas X was a popular Twitter meme creator before he posted "Old Town Road." To argue that anyone can upload their music and become the record holder for the longest Number 1 song on the Billboard Hot 100 misses the point that this did not happen for 20 million other aspiring performers. When streaming platforms allow everyone to upload their music, it complicates how to reach fans.

The second user-generated streaming platform is Band-Camp. If you follow local music, you have probably come across a band directing fans to their BandCamp page. Band-Camp provides users with a platform that emphasizes a band over discoverability. Most users do not visit BandCamp to find new music, but rather, bands direct fans to download their music through the site. Bands can charge whatever they want for downloads and the site allows free streams through the page. For instance, a local band in Fort Worth, Texas, Mean Motor Scooter, recently released a new album entitled "Mr. Sophistication" on BandCamp. Users can stream the album free or they can pay at least $5 to download the entire album. If they decide to download it, they can choose to spend more than $5 for the album. BandCamp also allows bands to sell merchandise through their platform. While there has not been the same type of fervent articles written about "BandCamp rockers" (I just coined the phrase), it does provide independent artists with a means to supplement their live performance income.

Music was the first popular cultural form to embrace streaming. However, the recording industry's embrace has never been public nor harmonious. Record labels contend streaming hurts artists and has moved the scourge from Napster to Spotify to YouTube. In fact, they deploy the phrase "value gap" to describe the gap between the value created by musicians and the amount YouTube pays for a stream.[21] Yet, streaming culture is now a fundamental part of listening practices, which generates profits for the recording industry. Unending consumption ensures music listeners have no choice, but to pay for every time they listen to a song.

NOTES

1. Michel Aglietta, *A Theory of Capitalist Regulation: The US Experience*, trans. David Fernbach, New edition (New York: Verso, 2001); Paul Smith, *Millennial Dreams: Contemporary Culture and Capital in the North*, The Haymarket Series (London; New York: Verso, 1997).
2. Kembrew McLeod, "MP3s Are Killing Home Taping: The Rise of Internet Distribution and Its Challenge to the Major Label Music Monopoly," *Popular Music and Society* 28, no. 4 (October 2005): 521-31.
3. Theodor W. Adorno, "The Form of the Phonograph Record," in *Essays on Music/Theodor W. Adorno*, ed. Theodor W. Adorno, Richard D. Leppert, and Susan H. Gillespie (Berkeley: University of California Press, 2002), 278.
4. Jonathan Sterne, *MP3: The Meaning of a Format* (Durham: Duke University Press, 2012).
5. Paul du Gay et al., *Doing Cultural Studies: The Story of the Sony Walkman*, 2nd ed. (Los Angeles: SAGE, 2013).
6. Monica Mercuri, "Spotify Reports First Quarterly Operating Profit, Reaches 96 Million Paid Subscribers," *Forbes*, February 6, 2019, Online edition, sec. Hollywood &

Entertainment, https://www.forbes.com/sites/monicamercuri/ 2019/02/06/spotify-reports-first-quarterly-operating-profit-reaches-96-million-paid-subscribers/.

7. Peter Lauria, "Universal Has A Big Stake In Beats That's Worth Nearly $500 Million," *BuzzFeed*, May 8, 2014, sec. Business, http://www.buzzfeed.com/peterlauria/universal-music-will-make-nearly-500-million-on-apples-beats.

8. Sony Corp. v. Universal City Studios, No. 81-1687 (United States Supreme Court January 17, 1984); Jessica Litman, *Digital Copyright* (Amherst: Prometheus Books, 2006); David Arditi, *ITake-Over: The Recording Industry in the Digital Era* (Lanham: Rowman & Littlefield Publishers, 2014).

9. Dallas Walker Smythe, "On the Audience Commodity and Its Work," in *Dependency Road: Communications, Capitalism, Consciousness, and Canada*, ed. Dallas Walker Smythe (Norwood: Ablex, 1981), 230-56; Christian Fuchs, "Dallas Smythe Today - The Audience Commodity, the Digital Labour Debate, Marxist Political Economy and Critical Theory. Prolegomena to a Digital Labour Theory of Value," *TripleC: Communication, Capitalism & Critique. Open Access Journal for a Global Sustainable Information Society* 10, no. 2 (September 19, 2012): 692-740; Sut Jhally, *The Codes of Advertising: Fetishism and the Political Economy of Meaning in the Consumer Society* (New York: St. Martin's Press, 1987).

10. David Arditi, "Digital Subscriptions: The Unending Consumption of Music in the Digital Era," in *Annual Meeting of the American Sociological Association* (Annual Meeting of the American Sociological Association, Seattle, WA, 2016).

11. Aaron Perzanowski and Jason Schultz, *The End of Ownership: Personal Property in the Digital Economy* (Cambridge: The MIT Press, 2016).

12. Robert Prey, "Nothing Personal: Algorithmic Individuation on Music Streaming Platforms," *Media, Culture & Society* 40, no. 7 (October 1, 2018): 1091, https://doi.org/10.1177/ 0163443717745147.

13. Pierre Bourdieu, *Distinction: A Social Critique of the Judgement of Taste* (Cambridge: Harvard University Press, 1984).

14. Nancy Weiss Hanrahan, "Hearing the Contradictions: Aesthetic Experience, Music and Digitization," *Cultural Sociology* 12, no. 3 (July 13, 2018): 289-302, https://doi.org/10.1177/1749975518776517; Nancy Weiss Hanrahan, "Digitized Music and the Aesthetic Experience of Difference," in *The Dialectic of Digital Culture*, ed. David Arditi and Jennifer Miller (Lanham: Lexington Books, 2019), 165–79.

15. Andrew Shapter, *Before the Music Dies*, 2006.

16. Gary Trust, "Imagine Dragons' 'Radioactive' Ends Record Billboard Hot 100 Run," *Billboard*, May 9, 2014, http://www.billboard.com/articles/columns/chart-beat/6084584/imagine-dragons-radioactive-ends-record-billboard-hot-100-run.

17. Arditi, "Digital Subscriptions: The Unending Consumption of Music in the Digital Era."

18. David Hesmondhalgh, Ellis Jones, and Andreas Rauh, "SoundCloud and Bandcamp as Alternative Music Platforms," *Social Media + Society* 5, no. 4 (October 1, 2019): 2056305119883429, https://doi.org/10.1177/2056305119883429.

19. Jon Caramanica, "The Rowdy World of Rap's New Underground," *The New York Times*, June 22, 2017, sec. Arts, https://www.nytimes.com/2017/06/22/arts/music/soundcloud-rap-lil-pump-smokepurrp-xxxtentacion.html.

20. Caramanica.

21. David Arditi, "Digital Hegemony: Net Neutrality, the Value Gap, and Corporate Interests," in *The Dialectic of Digital Culture*, ed. David Arditi and Jennifer Miller (Lanham: Lexington Books, 2019), 13–28; Emily Blake, "Services like YouTube Largely Blamed for the Music 'value Gap' in New Report," Digital News, Mashable, April 12, 2016, http://mashable.com/2016/04/12/music-value-gap/; Glenn Peoples, "War of Words: Labels and Trade Groups Target YouTube's 'Value Gap,'" *Billboard*, April 13, 2016, http://www.billboard.com/articles/business/7333110/war-of-words-labels-trade-groups-youtube-value-gap.

4

STREAMING FILM: SIMULTANEOUS RELEASE, CIRCUMVENTING CENSORSHIP, AND INDIES

Netflix changed the way we watch movies. However, Netflix did not change everything through its popular streaming app, but rather it changed movies through a mail delivery movie rental subscription service. From the privacy of your own home, you could subscribe, select your movies and have them delivered. Depending on your subscription level, you could have different numbers of DVDs checked-out at a time. When you returned a DVD, Netflix sent you the next movie on your list. In a few short years, Netflix (with some help from Redbox) killed the video rental store—mainly its biggest chain: Blockbuster. Today, the irony is Netflix is not a movie behemoth, but rather a television-streaming magnet (more on this in the next chapter). The subscription model eliminated the need to go to video rental stores and promises to change movie theater culture. Remember though: digital disruption causes more problems for distribution and retail than it does for content creators. Through streaming technology, the movie watching experience has changed and further entrenched unending consumption.

Before we write-off video rental stores entirely, I do have a nostalgia for it, but the nostalgia demonstrates the allure of unending consumption. On a Saturday night, my partner and I would often prepare for a movie-night-in by grabbing a bite to eat and stopping by Blockbuster. The store opened itself to browsing popular new releases on the walls in alphabetical order and older releases in the center of the store arranged by genre. The biggest hits took up the most shelf-space and were clearly the driving force behind movie rental consumption. Blockbuster encouraged customers to rent a "blockbuster" by including 50 copies of the DVD box, usually with every copy rented. Of course, the movie rentals were often loss leaders because there was more to buy at the store than movie rentals. As you waited in a long line on a Friday or Saturday night at Blockbuster, you meandered past popcorn, candy, soda, and movie merchandise. This created synthesis between movies and brands by allowing fans to rent *Lord of the Rings*, buy an Aragorn action figure, and *Lord of the Rings* branded popcorn. For the superfan, this enabled easy conspicuous consumption and surplus revenue for Blockbuster. Movie rental stores signified an event much the same way going to a movie theater is an event.

Unlike television, movies historically required the watcher to go somewhere, unless they watched a movie on television. However, aside from movies on HBO, Showtime or other premium subscription cable services, watching movies on television was a terrible experience because of commercials, censorship, and editing to fit television screen dimensions (before flat-screen TVs became universal). Commercials during movies are a double-edged sword: first, commercials are annoying; second, they come at inopportune moments because movies are not designed for commercial breaks. While there have always been "made-for-TV" movies, the moniker represents low-budget low-quality movies. Furthermore, before DVRs, you had to be ready for the start of the movie at a set time to at the very least tape the movie. As a result, movie-watchers willingly forked over $5 for a 24-hour rental to avoid the morass of watching movies on television. Yet, the shift to streaming movies changes this logic as we can consume seemingly infinite movies without leaving home.

Film was distinct from other cultural commodities because of its emphasis on the theater experience. However, streaming services eliminated the barriers that made movies singular events. This chapter explores the ways that simultaneous release, widescreen television, and made-for-*streaming* films changed the cultural position of film. Streaming movies makes movies more accessible, which could invigorate the independent movie scene (i.e. film produced by non-major studios). I discuss how websites such as Vimeo allow amateur filmmakers to distribute their ideas, but major film studios continue to foster inequality. Next, I explore how film content has changed because streaming service releases do not have to comply with the Motion Picture Association of America's (MPAA) moving picture board. The oligopoly of film studios and theater owners used the MPAA's rating system to censor content and keep independent films out of theaters. I argue streaming movies allows for a more democratic censorship regime, but the MPAA still controls the bulk of content produced. Finally, this chapter explores the changing nature of film collections in our everyday cultural milieu. I conclude by looking at how streaming movies helps create the system of unending consumption.

THE CHANGING FILM EXPERIENCE

Going to a movie theater provides an experience. Moviegoers experience the film the way the director intended for it to be scene. We perceive being enveloped by the film with a large screen and bone-rattling surround sound. We hear fellow moviegoers experience the film through laughter, silence, screeches, fleeting interjections, and applause. We smell popcorn and crave movie comfort foods (popcorn, candy, nachos, and soda) when they are not part of our typical diet. These experiences attract people to the theater despite the increasingly exorbitant price of admission. However, the changing home theater experience, in addition to streaming movie apps, promises to change the culture of movie watching.

Directors do not shoot movies to be viewed on televisions. This is most-notable before the flat screen television era. Tube televisions were nearly square with a 4:3 aspect ratio. Most films were shot for a widescreen rectangular projector with an aspect ratio of 1.85:1. In order for films to be available on television (cable, airwaves, or rentals), they needed to be edited; hence the "This film has been modified from its original version" message affixed to films on television. This began to change around 2000 when LCD flat panel televisions became available to the consumer market. These televisions contain a 1.78:1 or 16:9 aspect ratio. Flat panel televisions also tend to be larger than tube televisions and use a greater percentage of the screen. With the aspect ratio closer to theaters and larger screen sizes, flat panel televisions improved the movie watching experience at home. Flat panel digital TVs come equipped with software that automatically adjusts aspect ratio whereas analog tube televisions could never change aspect ratio. Following the Federal Communication Commission's switch to digital in June 2009, broadcasters can only broadcast digital signals. As a result, TV broadcasters transmit all movies in digital format and no longer transmit movies in modified form. Since films no longer have to be modified from their original form, they can be released for home consumption much sooner, if not simultaneously, depending on licensing issues.

The simultaneous release of films was once viewed by major film studios as a revenue killer. The basic political economy of the Hollywood film industry is to recoup revenue from the film through domestic United States consumption at movie theater box offices. They then rely on the secondary market to generate profits for their releases.[1] The secondary market of film includes international box offices, licensing to television, and rentals. Studio executives worry that simultaneously releasing a film in theaters and for watching at home will crush box office revenues—the source of revenue they rely on to recoup the cost of the film.[2]

Made-for-TV movies have traditionally been low-budget films that follow a formula. Hallmark Christmas movies provide the pinnacle example of made-for-TV movies. In them, the lead character (usually a woman) will find love by Christmas. It usually involves her going home to see family in a small town somewhere in the North (often playing with a Santa Claus and North Pole theme). The low budget and high-demand for getting in the "Christmas spirit" allow these films to generate revenue without box office revenues. However, streaming services changed the hesitancy of directors, producers, and studios to produce made-for-TV content.

Streaming services reinvented the made-for-TV model while rebranding them "original" movies. Amazon Studios produced its first streaming film, *The Stolen Child*, in 2008, but Amazon Studios did not catch-on for nearly a decade. Netflix produced its first original movie, *Beasts of No Nation*, in 2015. Netflix also began partnering with production companies to produce original movies, like Adam Sandler's Happy Madison Productions, in 2015. These movies rarely appear in theaters and have changed the way we think about streaming culture and the culture of streaming.

As more companies release streaming video platforms, movie watchers need to subscribe to more services. What began with Netflix and Amazon now includes original movies from Hulu, Disney+, HBO Max, and Apple+, among others. To watch any given film can require a subscription to any one of these services. So any avid movie watcher may feel the urge to subscribe to all of these services. This has been labeled the "streaming wars," but more on this in the next chapter. For now, it is important to think about how this changes movies and advances unending consumption. Whereas before the streaming era, people could go to a movie theater, rent from a video rental store, or watch a film on TV, there was little room for added revenue. But with unending consumption, our lives become entrenched in more and more subscriptions for targeted content.

If someone wants to watch a film on HBO Max, they have to subscribe for $14.99/month to watch one movie. They may be able to find an offer for a week or a month free, but they still have to provide credit card information. This same subscriber may be subscribed to Hulu, Disney+, Netflix and Amazon Prime. The most seductive part of the subscription model for the film industry is how many people forget they have subscriptions. In fact, Wells Fargo is so aware of our ubiquitous subscriptions to things we don't care about that they developed an app, Control Tower, to alert us to our monthly subscriptions. Control Tower tracks recurring payments and sorts them to remind users about these payments. The basic idea behind Wells Fargo's ad campaign for the app is people forget they subscribe to streaming services and this is a way to once again control your payments. However, corporations with streaming services see profits from us forgetting to unsubscribe.

When movie theaters shuttered in March 2020 due to the COVID-19 pandemic, the process of streaming movies accelerated. Without the ability to watch these new releases in the theaters, some film studios released their films through streaming platforms. For instance, Amazon began renting new release movies for $19.99 as "Prime Video Cinema." With the average price of a movie ticket in 2020 around $10, this works out to the cost of two tickets at a movie theater. However, this is only possible because people are used to watching movies at home. Indie movies did not have the same opportunities to switch their films from theaters to streaming as the major film studios and distributors, but some indie studios found a way around movie theaters. For instance, the independent film *St. Frances* created an online theater through its distributor, Oscilloscope. Moviegoers could purchase a $10 ticket to stream the film from the comfort of their own homes.[3] With wide-screen high-definition televisions as the industry standard, surround sound systems, and internet enabled televisions, streaming movies at home is a widely accepted cultural practice.

The COVID-19 lockdown created a new type of collective consumption. Watching a film at a theater provides a collective experience that makes people feel part of a community. At theaters, we hear others laugh, feel the silence of films like *A Quiet Place*, hear the person behind of us saying "don't go in there" during a horror film, or experience applause after a great film. In these moments we experience collective effervescence – an electric feeling experienced by groups of people. Collective effervescence is what makes us feel like part of something. Watching a film in a theater makes us feel part of a community, and we do not feel it at home. While we could not go out to see movies during the COVID-19 lockdown, we gained other forms of community in our socially distanced lives. Some people began streaming films at home while Zooming with friends.[4] Granted, while watching movies while Zooming doesn't provide the viewers with collective effervescence, it does reinforce or form social bonds. Many people already did similar activities before the pandemic if they lived far from friends and family, but so-called social distancing created new forms of sociality. These forms of cultural practice that arise during moments of crisis create long-term changes to the way we think about culture.

These are only the latest changes to the cinema experience. As more films become available streaming-first, theaters have had to find new ways to seduce movie viewers to visit theaters. With ticket prices doubling over the last two decades, theaters emphasized the moviegoing experience. Theaters went from cramming customers in like sardines to stadium seating to luxury recliners and assigned seats. Many movie theaters began serving alcohol. And theaters increasingly trend towards theater restaurants with the rise of chains like Studio Movie Grill and the Movie Tavern. For parents paying for babysitters, these movie restaurants' ability to kill two birds with one stone by shortening date nights to the movie theater and reducing the cost of babysitters.

Regardless of the changes, the main movies available for consumption continue to be from major Hollywood studios. What about independent films? If we're watching at home, we should be able to consume more independent films that could never make it to the theaters.

INDEPENDENT STREAMING

A bright spot in the streaming era is the development and distribution of independent content. Streaming platforms allow independent film directors to make new content outside of the major studio, distribution and theater oligopoly. However, just as music streaming services benefit the major record labels, popular streaming services give an advantage to major film studios. The case in point above is the story of

"Saint Frances" during the COVID-19 pandemic. The producers of "Saint Frances" could not get Amazon, Netflix or any other streaming service to carry the release, so they had to utilize an independent platform for its release. These platforms provide opportunities for independent filmmakers, but they do not allow these filmmakers to compete with major studios. Furthermore, these independent movie apps are not available on most smart TVs and media devices like Roku. While streaming platforms disrupt the movie distribution chain and allow users to share content, they do so while reinforcing the strength of major studios and selling (i.e. sharing) user data.

YouTube paved the way for users to upload their produced content online. Launched independently in 2005, Google purchased the video uploading site in 2006. YouTube provided users a simple platform to upload videos online. However, controversy always followed YouTube from Prince demanding the takedown of a video of a toddler dancing to his song "Let's Go Crazy"[5] to Billboard's initial refusal to count YouTube streams in their charts.[6] Film, Television, and music copyright owners have initiated a number of challenges against YouTube because they desire stricter protections and more lucrative licenses. Google has done everything it can to stay within the law, but that often is not good enough for content owners. When a video violates copyright, the owners can demand YouTube remove the content through a Digital Millennium Copyright Act (DMCA) takedown notice. These notices require a digital service to remove infringing material, but copyright owners often complain these notices allow infringers to pop-up continually and fighting them is like playing whack-a-mole. The bigger problems come for independent film producers to upload their films on YouTube. If they use a film clip or music for which they do not receive copyright clearance to use, then the copyright owner can issue a DMCA takedown notice. This provides a blank check for

the major studios and major labels to crush independent producers because there is no surefire way to defeat a takedown
notice. Just like clearing copyrighted content is expensive,
fighting the Culture Industry's lawyers is costly. User-generated
content faces an uphill battle during unending consumption as
major corporations in the Culture Industry restrict access to the
expansion of the means of consumption.

Vimeo provides a platform for independent filmmakers.
Launched in 2004, before YouTube, program developers
created the platform for filmmakers to disseminate their work
to the world.[7] With aspiring filmmakers in mind, the platform
has Vimeo Video School to train film directors, producers,
videographers, etc. As an independent distribution platform,
Vimeo fosters creativity and experimentation with video.
These artsy films range from a couple of minutes to a couple
of hours. They allow directors to break-free from the
creativity-stifling demands of working for major studios and
big-time producers. The short nature of the content allows
directors to explore the extent of their imaginations and this
could help movie watchers change their expectations for film
content. Since Vimeo records big data in the background,
information about consumption can lead to trend changes in
mainstream movies. However, when the deployment of big
data shows new trends, it doesn't mean the directors or producers who initiate the trends benefit with studio release of
their films. Studios use consumption information to change
mainstream films, not change mainstream filmmakers.

For the longer content on Vimeo, users must pay to rent or
purchase films. Similar to Bandcamp (discussed in Chapter 3),
filmmakers can set the purchase and/or rental price of their
films. This gives control to the filmmakers to determine the
value of their films. However, there is a very short list of
filmmakers who successfully turned Vimeo video productions
to fame and fortune or even a decent salary. In an effort to

raise the prestige of films on the platform, Vimeo launched the Vimeo Festival & Awards show. Recently, the platform collaborated with Sundance Film Festival to stream short films for the festival. However, user-generated films have not had cultural success.

Why is it important to give independent films a chance? First, independent films develop new directions for popular culture. Second, and I think more importantly, Hollywood films lack diversity. Beginning in 2015, the film community posted about #OscarsSoWhite. This Twitter hashtag aims to demonstrate the racial inequalities in the biggest award committee for film.[8] When people of color are given starring roles in Hollywood, they are forced to play a stereotype from playing a maid for African-American women to playing a terrorist for Muslim men.[9] Hollywood stifles the ability for people of color to breakthrough as the every woman. Aziz Ansari addresses these issues in a critical episode of *Master of None* entitled "Indians on TV."[10] From *Short Circuit* to a popchips commercial starring Ashton Kutcher, directors and producers find it acceptable to use brown face to have white actors play Indian parts. Blackface, brownface, and negative stereotypes proliferate in Hollywood, and without a vibrant independent film scene, there will be inequality in the roles people of color can play. Finally, Hollywood success breeds circular thinking about what successful films and actors look like. From conceptions about why certain movies do well at the box office to which actors should be cast for specific roles, conventional wisdom perpetuates the status quo. Independent films create new opportunities for filmmakers. For instance, Jordan Peele's psychological horror film *Get Out* (2017)[11] was an independent film (though it was still distributed by Universal Studios) that smartly delved into racism by a Black director, which does not exist among major studio films. Since streaming can meander around the institutional logics of major Hollywood studios, it brings the as-yet-unrealized potential of becoming a platform for independent films.

Streaming culture thrives on consumption of major studio film projects. Yet, streaming platforms affect the culture of film. One-way streaming platforms change film production is in the type of content deemed acceptable in films.

CENSORSHIP

In the 2006 documentary *This Film Is Not Yet Rated*, Kirby Dick explores the institutional censorship mandated by the Motion Pictures Association of America (MPAA).[12] Dick levels a scathing critique of the major film studios' oligarchic power over what movies theaters can show. Basically, an NC-17 rating is a film killer because most theaters will not play the films. Most soon-to-be-blockbusters do not want anything higher than a PG-13 rating because an R rating will lower box office sales. The MPAA has an anonymous rating board supposedly composed of parents of young children. While Dick demonstrates the parental requirement to be false, he also outlines a disturbing practice of hiring people for these boards that have no formal qualifications to review films. Furthermore, the MPAA applies their standards unevenly to films depending on whether majors or indies produce the film. Ironically, Netflix's film production company helped to produce the film, which will make sense below. Whereas the MPAA runs movie theaters like a cartel system, streaming permits the opportunity for open production systems that use alternative forms of ratings or skips the practice entirely.

The MPAA regulates everything from the specific number of times a profane word can be used to the length of an orgasm.[13] This regulation occurs outside of the state, which makes it unaccountable to the democratic populace. As Dick shows, none of this regulation is transparent. Independent film directors do not receive feedback that describes why their film received a specific rating. However, major studios receive a report describing exactly why a film received a rating to give them the option to edit the film. This is critical information for directors, otherwise they can receive the NC-17 kiss of death or miss the PG-13 blockbuster sweet spot. But the material censored also has no expertise behind it. Today, the MPAA uses "parents" as the guardians of morality, but at different times in US film history, different groups have used film censorship to model their morality to the populace.[14] In the United Kingdom, the British Board of Film Classification uses experts in fields such as psychology and media studies to rate films. However, Hollywood's position as the biggest film producer in the world gives the MPAA's censors outsized control over film content. If Hollywood produces most films, then those films must meet the MPAA's requirements. And theaters will only play films that are rated by the MPAA. A democratic platform would be transparent, would utilize expertise, and would be accountable to elected officials and the citizen body.

Streaming platforms have the potential to crack the censorship cartel. Netflix, Amazon, Hulu, and HBO Max resist the MPAA's rating system. As I mentioned above, Netflix co-produced *This Film Is Not Yet Rated*, and it feels a little self-serving for the subscription service to critique the major studio rating system. However, this does not mean these streaming platforms do not utilize rating systems. In fact, they all have parental controls, which allow users to limit content in their homes. Netflix uses a combination of MPAA ratings for films already rated and the TV Parental Guidelines for their original content. The biggest difference between MPAA ratings and the TV Parental Guidelines is the TV Parental Guidelines allow producers to determine their ratings. People can file a complaint to the TV Parental Guidelines Monitoring Board if they feel something is misrated. This type of censorship is bottom-up instead of top-down, at least on paper.

Since streaming platforms do not necessarily use the MPAA's rating system, it presents the potential to crack open the American film censorship regime. Filmmakers can approach Netflix or Amazon Prime to produce their films and avoid the hurdles of entering theaters. While this frees directors from limiting the number of times they drop the F-bomb, it may work to change the MPAA rating system as theaters begin to miss out on quality films that release streaming first. However, we always must remember Netflix and Amazon are private companies and there is no transparency in their censorship practices. They will not produce films that impact their bottom lines or contradict their brands. Streaming culture does not create an open democratic system of film ratings, we must demand it.

NO MORE DVD COLLECTIONS

My family just moved into a new home. We've been moving a bulky home theater system with us for around 11 years. This home theater system has wired 5.1 surround sound and a built-in DVD player. In the new home we dealt with two questions about the system. First, what do we do with the speaker wires? Second, where do we put the system's receiver? In the end, we moved the system into our office and we'll wait until it makes sense to buy a new home theater system that works in our space. The biggest debate we had about the system's move to the office revolved around the question: how will we watch DVDs? After some thought, we discovered we really don't watch DVDs. Outside of the occasional trip to

Redbox or cartoons from the library, we don't use a DVD player all that much. Because we can stream most movies into our home with the click of a button, we no longer have a reason to use a DVD player.

The process of leaving DVD consumption to the home office provides me with anxiety. When we decided to hook up the home theater system in the office, I figured I would hook up all our old technology: home theater, Wii, Xbox 360, Sega Genesis emulator and a VCR. This was a big moment. Now I could have my old drum VHS tapes next to my desk and play them whenever I got the itch. Then I realized the TV doesn't have enough hook-ups for everything, and the VCR took its place in the closet. Now I can only watch my drum videos when I hook-up the VCR, which honestly won't happen.

The same goes for our sizable DVD collection. We have dozens of DVDs displayed nicely on shelves, but I can count the number of times we've played these DVDs. We're not people who watch DVDs after we watch them once, except for our son's cartoons. Streaming movies works for us in this way. If a film is available on one of our subscription services, we can easily stream the movie. If the film is not available, we can usually rent it through Amazon or FandangoNOW. However, this brings us back to unending consumption.

There are occasions where we watch the same movies repeatedly on our streaming services. Our son is obsessed with *Star Wars*. We've watched most episodes multiple times. His obsession began before Disney+ launched. At first, we borrowed the DVDs from our next-door neighbors, so I could catch my wife up to speed and determine what was age appropriate. When they didn't have an episode available, we would rent it from Amazon Prime. In Fall 2019, we decided it was time for him to watch the movies. We watched a couple on various streaming services, but as the launch of Disney+ approached, Disney pulled the licenses to rent or stream for free all of the *Star Wars* movies. We waited for Disney+ to launch and subscribed immediately. My son quickly caught up on the episodes he hadn't seen and now he has seen each movie multiple times. But I wonder at what point the $6.99/month will exceed the value of purchasing DVDs for the movies and TV shows he watches on Disney+. For instance, I can buy the *Star Wars* box set for $50 or a five-month subscription. After a year, Disney earns $69.99 from me, a sum I've never spent on movies in a year (including going to the movies) and I receive access to other Disney content through my Hulu Live subscription (i.e. "cable"). But if we stop subscribing to Disney+, the movies are gone.

While we may get our money's worth out of a Disney+ subscription, how does this expand the means of consumption? Remember that with unending consumption, the question is not whether people receive their money's worth in a physical media environment, but whether people spend more under the streaming regime than before it. Would we spend $70/year on DVDs? Or would the movies just be unavailable? Most importantly, does the revenue from Disney+ outpace revenue from DVD sales at their zenith? This is an empirical question, but Disney does not make the data readily available to answer this question. My guess is revenue from subscriptions far exceeds revenue from DVDs with higher profits from the lack of physical product to make and to distribute the discs. This greatly expands the means of consumption.

DVDs may collect dust, but they are always there. Streaming culture enables us to expect that movies will always be available at our fingertips, and we pay for it, too.

CONCLUSION

While bigger in the sports broadcast world, pay-per-view movies became available through cable and satellite television providers in the 1980s.[15] These systems fostered what Vincent Mosco termed the "pay-per society" in which companies "explored the range of opportunities to advance the commodification of information."[16] The emphasis here is the commodification of information. A cable subscription already commodified watching television (discussed in the next chapter), but a subscription enabled access to everything. In the political economy of the pay-per society, cable companies whet subscribers' appetites for content on the basic subscription level, but deliver profit from subscribers who want more content. When people realize their subscriptions only give them censored movies with commercials from the catalog (i.e. older movies), they see the convenience of access to hit films or XXX-rated films through an additional fee.

Before major studios started releasing films online for an additional fee during COVID-19, Amazon provided pay-per streaming rentals. This exemplifies another aspect of unending consumption as it relates to the pay-per society. My wife and I replaced our trips to Blockbuster with evenings at home streaming movies. As early adopters of Netflix, we grew accustomed to their early streaming service. We felt as though the world of movies was available at our fingertips. Then Amazon Prime Video began streaming more videos. Instead of licensing all films to both services, film studios decided to have Hulu, Amazon, and Netflix, among others, compete for licenses. As Chuck Tryon demonstrates, "despite claims about a giant celestial megaplex in the computing cloud, in which we will have comparatively easy access to the history of film, what we will have instead is something closer to a range of competing miniplexes."[17] The result is uneven access and as more companies offer streaming services (Apple TV, Disney+, HBO Max), which makes it more difficult to find movies. We now remain firmly in the pay-per society built on unending consumption. My wife and I often stay home, forgoing the new releases available at the nearby Redbox, with a plan to stream from one of our services. However, after 30 minutes of searching through films, we find the good new releases are only available for rental or purchase. As a result, we end-up either watching television shows or paying Amazon $4.99 for 48 hours of access. We grew accustomed to pay-per-view through video-on-demand features when we were Time Warner Cable subscribers. Why is this unending consumption? Because we continue subscribing AND we pay-per-view. If we jumped in a time machine to the 1980s, we might have a cable subscription with a premium channel, but our additional consumption would be limited. Now we have multiple subscriptions, and on movie night, we still can't find something to watch, so we pay for it.

While streaming film may change how we watch movies, it does not disrupt Hollywood's power—it expands the power of the major film studios. We spend more on streaming films, provide our data to movie studios and streaming services, and remain embedded in systems that limit democratic thought and foster inequality.

NOTES

1. Vincent Mosco, *The Pay-Per Society: Computers and Communication in the Information Age* (Norwood: Praeger, 1989).
2. Chuck Tryon, *On-Demand Culture: Digital Delivery and the Future of Movies*, None edition (New Brunswick: Rutgers University Press, 2013), 37-40.

3. Ann Hornaday, "What Is a Movie? With Theaters Shutter-ing, the Question Gets Real.," *Washington Post*, March 19, 2020, sec. Perspective, https://www.washingtonpost.com/entertainment/what-is-a-movie-with-theaters-shuttering-the-question-gets-real/2020/03/18/930f16ec-6874-11ea-9923-57073adce27c_story.html.

4. Joe Berkowitz, "Watching Movies with Friends on Zoom or Google Hangouts Can Make Quarantine Less Dreary," *Fast Company*, March 20, 2020, https://www.fastcompany.com/90479962/watching-movies-with-friends-on-zoom-or-google-hangouts-can-make-quarantine-less-dreary.

5. Greg Sandoval, "Mother Protects YouTube Clip by Suing Prince," *CNET*, October 30, 2007, http://news.cnet.com/8301-10784_3-9807555-7.html.

6. David Arditi, "Billboard Plays Catch-up to YouTube's Dominance," *The Tennessean*, March 9, 2020, Online edi-tion, sec. Opinion, https://www.tennessean.com/story/opini on/2020/03/09/billboard-catches-up-to-youtube-dominance/5005889002/.

7. Nick O'Leary, "Vimeo: YouTube's Better-Looking Little Brother," *Information Today; Medford* (Medford: Infor-mation Today, Inc., November 2013).

8. Reggie Ugwu, "The Hashtag That Changed the Oscars: An Oral History," *The New York Times*, February 6, 2020, sec. Movies, https://www.nytimes.com/2020/02/06/movies/oscar ssowhite-history.html.

9. David Grazian, *Mix It Up: Popular Culture, Mass Media, and Society*, 2nd ed. (New York: W. W. Norton, Incorpo-rated, 2017); Brent Lang, "Viola Davis Knows What's Wrong With Hollywood... and How to Fix It," *Variety* (blog), September 4, 2018, https://variety.com/2018/film/features/viola-davis-widows-pay-gap-hollywood-1202924041/.

10. Eric Wareheim, *Indians on TV*, Comedy (3 Arts Entertain-ment, Alan Yang Pictures, Fremulon, 2015).

11. Jordan Peele, *Get Out*, Film (Universal Pictures, Blumhouse Productions, QC Entertainment, 2017).

12. Kirby Dick, *This Film Is Not Yet Rated*, Documentary (Independent Film Channel (IFC), Netflix, British Broad-casting Corporation (BBC), 2006).

13. Dick.

14. Jennifer Lynn Miller, "Diminished Citizenship: A Genealogy of the Development of 'Soft Citizenship' at the Intersection of US Mass and Political Culture" (Dissertation, Fairfax, George Mason University, 2014), http://mars.gmu.edu/handle/1920/8857.
15. Tryon, *On-Demand Culture*.
16. Mosco, *The Pay-Per Society*, 27.
17. Tryon, *On-Demand Culture*, 32.

5

STREAMING TV: THE GOLDEN AGE OF TV AND FLOW INTERRUPTED

In 2013, Netflix had a monumental year by releasing three original series changing television and streaming for the foreseeable future. While Hulu began releasing original television series as early as 2011, these shows did not receive the viewership or Emmy Award recognition of the Netflix series. These shows heralded what has been called the "golden age of television." They also fundamentally changed the content available on streaming platforms as these platforms shifted to television series subscribers could binge over movies—the latter became premium content as described in Chapter 4.

We've also entered what has been termed the "streaming wars" as tech companies and television networks try to exploit the open market for streaming TV. As I write this, NBC just launched Peacock, a platform to stream NBC shows, Universal Studios' movies, and original content. Peacock is the quintessential example of unending consumption. Currently, I can watch NBC-Universal content on other streaming platforms from Hulu to Netflix. Viewers can also watch NBC over-the-air and via cable. However, NBC-Universal has begun to withdraw their licenses to stream films from other platforms. Peacock has tiered service. The free tier is ad-supported and allows viewers to watch content available through cable, broadcast, or other platforms. The Premier plan is $4.99/month and gives subscribers access to originals and movies, but still with commercials. The Premier Plus plan is $9.99/month and has the added benefit of being ad-free. NBC-Universal hopes to rope people in with original series, like *Brave New World*, but it is ironic that Peacock would have "original" content considering NBC is a TV network! Why doesn't NBC air *Brave New World* at 10pm/9pm Central on Tuesdays? NBC sees more revenue potential in a streaming service than the broadcast television model. Peacock also created rebellions among NBC's affiliate stations, which fear they will lose viewers due to the app. The initial launch of Peacock came with a *30 Rock* TV special, but many of the TV affiliates refused to air the show in protest (this is a strange move because that forces *30 Rock* fans to download the app). Peacock is one example of the ever-expanding television streaming services that lead to unending consumption.

The past several years have been called the "golden age of television." This chapter explores the reasons why television is so great in the streaming era. First, I trace a short history from VHS/Betamax tapes through DVRs to streaming. A key term explored in this chapter is "flow" – the way television patterns help determine our consumption. Since we are no longer beholden to broadcast schedules, streaming interrupts flow, which allows new cultural forms to develop alongside streaming television. Then I discuss the way streaming services change the political economy of television. In the next section, I discuss binge-watching. One key to how our television culture has changed is the fact that we binge shows like a long movie. Next, I explore how cultural innovations associated with streaming technology developed the golden age of television. Finally, I consider the way streaming television creates new modes of cultural interaction in the conclusion to this chapter.

FROM VHS TO DVR: TRYING TO WATCH A SHOW

Keeping up with the Kardashians is easy because we can record their shows or find it streaming somewhere online. Following a series took dedication before streaming. If your show was on at 8pm on Tuesdays, you had to be home to catch the next episode. If you missed an episode, you may be able to catch it out of sequence during a rerun[1]—and those darn reruns could ruin your Tuesday if you rearranged things to be . If you missed an episode with a y have to wait for the producers S or DVD. In the streaming era, t cause they are omnipresent online hnological shifts, television produ ate elements from serial dram

W d Betamax and VHS tapes (respectively) in the mid 1970s, the television watching experience changed with the video cassette recorder (VCR). Being able to record live television created the opportunity for time-shifting—being able to watch television recordings at different times. In a landmark case known as the "Betamax Case" (*Sony Corp. of America v. Universal City Studios, Inc.*), the Supreme Court of the United States ruled in favor of Sony assigning "fair use" to recording television programming for private use. Television viewers could now record their favorite shows and go do other things at the time those shows air. But many people couldn't program their VCRs. There was an ongoing joke throughout the VCR era that you needed a degree to program the time on a VCR. Many VCRs would flash 12:00 after a power outage. While programming the time was difficult, programming it to record at a specified time was event trickier. As a result, time-shifting worked great to catch-up on missed shows in theory, but in practice it was quite difficult.

TiVo launched the first digital video recorder (DVR) in 1999 at the annual Consumer Electronics Show. These digital boxes permitted users to record live television in digital format. The digital interface provided easier programming options and easier search functions as they catalogued similar to Windows' file folders. Furthermore, TiVo provided hard drive space to store shows, movies, and other programming in one place. I remember one friend's house growing up where they had a room of bookcases filled with VHS tapes, all home recorded from television programming. In my own home, we would record and re-record on the same VHS tapes often leading to tapes being mislabeled. A number of popular culture references to mislabeling VHS tapes as people mislabel sex tapes and other people end up watching them. Mislabeled VHS tapes could be catastrophic.

DVRs developed around the same time cable companies transitioned to digital cable boxes. Eventually DVRs and cable boxes merged into one device. At the same time, cable companies expanded their video on demand broadcasting options. Video on demand (VOD) developed out of the pay-per-view model, but over time, this feature developed to allow cable subscribers to watch content that airs on any channel after the original airing.[2] In a way, VOD made DVRs obsolete at the same time cable boxes put DVRs in every subscriber's home. One big difference existed between DVR recordings and VOD: DVR allows users to fast-forward commercials whereas video on demand forces subscribers to watch them. Since commercials are the most important stream of revenue for television producers, video on demand forces viewers to continue to produce value.[3] VOD marks the beginning of streaming television because users stream content from a central server without storing it locally.

Raymond Williams discussed "flow" in television recordings as a "*sequence* or set of alternative sequences" of events, "which are. . . available in a single dimension and in a single operation."[4] Flow is both technological and cultural because the technology restricted how we view television and structured our everyday experience. For instance, a typical east coast broadcast network has the following sequence: 5-7pm news; 7-8pm game shows or Hollywood gossip; 8-11pm prime time television; 11pm news; 11:35pm late night television variety shows. During the broadcast television era, everyone experienced this flow. Even within the prime-time slot, sitcoms and police shows typically aired 8-10pm and more adult-oriented dramas held the 10-11pm time slot. It structured when people ate dinner, washed and put the kids to sleep, and put ourselves to sleep. The broadcast era severely limited the types of content available at any given time. The flow of TV programming was cultural in both senses discussed in this book. It created cultures around consumption at the same time it affected the way viewers make meaning of the world around them.

Since television programming creates audiences, which are sold to advertisers, television stations try to maximize audience retention through flow. They will place a very popular show between two not-so popular shows marketed to the same audience to tempt the audience into watching the network longer. TGIF was a great example. Thank God Its Friday (TGIF) was a sequence programmed by ABC geared toward whole family television. The main shows for TGIF in the late 1980s and 1990s included *Full House* and *Family*

Matters. ABC would then include other shows such as *Dinosaurs* to attract more similar viewers. This also proved an effective strategy to start new shows such as *Sabrina the Teenage Witch* and *Boy Meets World.* These shows made Friday nights great for families at home. Flow happens within shows, too. For instance, a news program provides a specific sequence that teases some of the information (weather, sports) that will keep viewers watching the entire broadcast. Television shows provide strong hooks early in the shows to interest the audience in the outcome of the show.

DVRs and streaming interrupted television flow. These technologies provide viewers with the opportunity to skip commercials and watch TV shows on their schedule. Then major broadcast companies Disney (which owns ABC and ESPN), NBC, and News Corporation partnered to develop Hulu, which launched in 2007. While networks began to offer television shows through their websites after their initial airing, Hulu provided a platform for these recordings. Soon Hulu made many forms of digital recordings obsolete as subscribers could log-in and watch most recent shows without a subscription. Time-shifting hit a new point as the networks themselves released shows without anchoring them to any given timeslot.

POLITICAL ECONOMY OF STREAMING TELEVISION

Unlike music, movies and video games, broadcast television's primary income stream comes from commercials. People watch TV shows, specific demographic groups are attracted to certain television programming, and TV producers sell those audiences to advertisers. This is the system media theorist Dallas Smythe called the audience commodity.[5] In turn, the audience commodity holds value for television networks. This is why commercials during golf tournaments sell Rolexes and high-end cars, soap operas sell laundry detergent and diapers, and news broadcasts sell life insurance. By defining an audience by a demographic group, television networks secure a higher rate of profit for their broadcasts because they ensure the right people watch the ads. Different audiences have different amounts of expendable income and different purchasing power. This explains why golf could have a small audience, but still secure broadcasting and high-dollar advertisements. But what happens when we no longer watch ads? First, advertisements proliferate within the show. Second, we pay for the programming through subscriptions. Third, streaming services "share" our personal data with third parties. While streaming culture means we do not watch as many commercials, the value of audiences continues to increase through unending consumption.

DVRs and streaming supposedly killed commercials by allowing users to fast-forward through them. One day in my Introduction to Popular Culture class, my students ridiculed me for watching commercials. When I explained that I watch on Hulu Live and many shows, live recorded, and VOD, required me to watch commercials. Their reply: use an ad-blocker. This was an entirely circular argument because I watch on a Roku, not my computer. However, much to their chagrin a week later, I referenced a commercial and almost everyone had seen the commercial—turns out they do watch commercials. Yes, we can work our way around commercials, but we still end up watching them. DVRs, streaming platforms, ad-blockers all help us to avoid commercials, but they do not eliminate the advertising logic that bolsters television consumption.

Networks and advertisers are acutely aware viewers avoid commercials, and this has always been a problem. During commercials viewers use the opportunity to use the restroom,

get a snack, or channel surf. Part of the reason why the content industry sued Sony over the Betamax was because VCRs
allowed viewers to fast-forward commercials. In response,
brands began using product placement within shows. Product
placement also worked on premium cable networks such as
HBO and Showtime, which even though they did not have
commercials, they could cash-in on the audience commodity.
My favorite product placement is Diet Coke in the Showtime
series *Weeds*.[6] In the show, the protagonist Nancy Botwin
almost always carries a can of Diet Coke perfectly displayed
for the camera. While *Weeds* aired on Showtime, a premium
station you pay extra for to avoid commercials, the network
raked in revenue from Diet Coke. *Weeds'* producers recognized their target audience was PTA moms dying for a calorie-
free caffeine fix. At the other end of the spectrum, MTV blurs
t-shirts, hats, beverage cans, etc. for product brands that don't
pay for the product placement. Computer monitors present
the ultimate advertising platform, and they seem natural. The
Apple logo became ubiquitous in TV shows and movies, these
blend in seamlessly because monitors have logos. However,
Microsoft did not have a parallel logo since Windows systems
were in Dells, HPs, etc. Then Microsoft started using the
Windows logo on the back of monitors as product placement
in TV shows and movies.

While product placements work well in fictional shows
based in our world, how do fantasy shows do product
placement? For companies like Disney, the shows become
advertisements for the products. Disney built an empire where
merchandising is as important as commercials. When my son
started watching Disney Junior, it occurred to me there was
very little advertising. Often, instead of the typical 7-8 minutes
of commercials during a show, Disney Junior only has a
couple commercials between shows. Part of this is a relic of
Disney being a premium cable subscription, but the branding

of the show is more important. *Mickey Mouse Clubhouse* sells the idea of Disney and can attract parents to Disney parks. For *Doc McStuffins*, Disney created veterinary toys for kids to check their stuffed animals. *PJ Masks* and *Vampirina* have action figures. In the Disney universe, television and film content are moments for marketing merchandise and theme parks.

During the streaming era, audiences pay for TV content through subscriptions. For instance, I can watch *Friends* on Netflix for $8.99/month for two years and never watch another show on Netflix. After I'm in for $215.76, I stop subscribing and I never have access again. As I write this, the complete series of *Friends* on DVD costs $80. Not only would I pay nearly three times more to watch Friends on Netflix, but Netflix can lose their license at any time. In fact, this happened after HBO Max purchased the rights to stream *Friends*—more on this below. But how many people would actually purchase the *Friends* complete series for $80? Likely, far fewer than would watch the series on Netflix. Again, this is unending consumption. We subscribe to a service and spend exponentially more on the content than we would in the analog era. Once we start, we can't stop.

Unending consumption doesn't stop with a subscription to one streaming service. We don't subscribe to only one streaming service because we are caught in the streaming wars. I brought *Friends* up not because I am a *Friends* fanatic (I'm not, and I haven't seen an episode since the 1990s), but because of its streaming journey. Netflix made a splash when it canceled its popular Marvel TV shows in 2018 but renewed its license for *Friends* for $80 million—only to lose the license to HBO Max one year later. Let's say you were on Season 4 of *Friends* when Netflix's license ended and HBO Max launched. In order to finish the series, you subscribe to HBO Max, but it is doubtful that you cancel your subscription to Netflix. Now you pay $8.99/month for Netflix *and* $14.99/month for HBO

Max. For $24/month you then have access to two streaming services. But you probably already pay $8.99/month for Amazon Prime Video, you may subscribe to Disney+ for $6.99/month, etc. More importantly, you may still be sub-scribed to a cable service that runs $50-$100/month. In the streaming era, many subscribers cut the proverbial cord by canceling their cable subscriptions. Our house cut cord, but we subscribe to Hulu Live for live television. Here's where cord-cutting becomes unending consumption – i.e. it expands the means of consumption. Hulu Live does not include AMC, Viacom networks, and much more. As longtime fans of *The Walking Dead*, my wife and I faced a decision when we subscribed to Hulu Live, give up watching *The Walking Dead*, purchase the season through Amazon, or subscribe to AMC for $4.99/month. We decided to purchase the season on Amazon, but this year AMC purchased the license to air the BBC show *Killing Eve* in America. So far, we've resisted watching *Killing Eve* Season 3, but it looks increasingly economical to subscribe to AMC after the next season of *The Walking Dead* begins. The list of subscriptions continues to grow while I still watch the same amount of television.

Even though we watch far fewer commercials in the streaming era, the audience is still a commodity. But the audience's commoditization remains obscured through pri-vacy policies that once again discuss "sharing" user data. During the analog era of television, TV networks, producers, and advertisers had a difficult time knowing who watched which shows. Nielsen Media Research developed methods to record media viewing in the 1930s for radio. At first these were social scientific surveys, which polled listeners to understand radio consumption. In 1950, Nielsen began monitoring television viewing. Nielsen developed a TV set meter that plugged into viewers' televisions to record viewing habits. Nielsen chose these viewers based on demographic information, which could be statistically representative of the broader population. Viewers with set monitors were paid by Nielsen to use these invasive devices. However, there was no telling who was watching any given show. Eventually, Nielsen developed more invasive monitors to better record demographic information and viewing habits. The turn to digital cable changed all of this as cable boxes became media research recording devices. Additionally, cable companies began to require a cable box for every TV. The more data TV networks and producers have about viewers, the more directly they can sell audiences to advertisers because they can more precisely address audience tastes. With each new technology, TV producers, networks, and advertisers developed new ways to monitor viewing, which increases the value of the audience commodity.

The streaming era creates a new level of data for TV producers and networks to sell to advertisers. Streaming platforms not only collect demographic information about viewers, they can figure out viewers' other tastes through tracking cookies.[7] These cookies are lines of code that become embedded on computers, tablets, or phones that record information about sites you visit and send the information back to the company that installed the code on your machine. These are massive privacy breaches we allow to monitor our internet browsing habits. Then streaming platforms can sell these data to different advertisers and other businesses. Technology enthusiasts call this "big data." The euphemism implies the large amount of information collected by organizations. The trick to big data is the more information collected about people's habits and demographics, the more patterns that become readily available through analysis of the data. For instance, data companies may identify a difference in beverage choices between people who watch *Friends* on HBO Max in the morning versus those who watch it in the evening. They may be of the exact same demographic group, but the one data point may show something valuable about beverage choices. While HBO Max doesn't have commercials and it can't place a new product in the show, HBO Max can sell that information to beverage companies and those companies can use that information in different ways to market to these groups.

Then streaming platforms use the same data to market back to viewers what they may want to watch. Netflix sends reminders to finish watching shows. Hulu emails subscribers about shows they may like. Furthermore, streaming platforms have algorithms that make recommendations based on your viewing interests. One day I clicked on my sister's Netflix profile only to be surprised by the great shows I never knew existed. Part of the problem is programmers do not know how to make sense of divergent interests on one account in my house. My son watches *Super Wings*, while my wife and I watch *Ozark*. This leads to a weird divergence between children's shows and adult content. Subscribers may appreciate the alerts and the recommendations may be perfect, but the goal isn't only to whet viewers' appetites. Rather, streaming platforms make suggestions based on big data to further lump groups of viewers together thereby making the audience commodity more valuable.

While streaming platforms transformed the political economy of television, streaming did not disrupt it. Advertising remains the principle way television networks fund TV shows, but advertising becomes increasingly subtle. The subtlety of advertising is enabled by violating subscribers' privacy. We consent to the changes as we subscribe to an increasing number of streaming platforms. However, the basic culture of TV viewing has changed as we binge TV instead of watching it at scheduled times.

BINGE-WATCHING

In the summer of 2011, I binged my first television series. At the time, it seemed like a herculean effort as my wife and I watched the first six seasons of *Grey's Anatomy*. As I write this, *Grey's Anatomy* finished its 16th season and I have no doubt someone is working their way through all 16 seasons. Morning, noon, and night we streamed *Grey's* hoping to catch-up before the start of Season 7. Of course, we made it with no problem, but that was just the beginning of our streaming binges. In Tanya Horeck, Mareike Jenner, and Tina Kendall's "On binge-watching: Nine critical propositions," they distinguish binge-watching as the following:

> *what distinguishes binge-watching from garden variety television viewing is the number of episodes viewed in one sitting. However, the question of what viewers define as 'bingeing' is likely to shift significantly depending on a range of factors, including age, occupation and family situation. What remains stable is that binge-watching is always understood as self-determined viewing: It is the viewer who decides when to watch and what to watch, not the broadcasting schedule.*[8]

To binge-watch a TV show is to watch the show at your own rate, but faster than a network schedule would allow. While binge-watching as a concept tends to be overused and underdefined in what constitutes a time period for binge-watching,[9] it remains a useful term if only because of its cultural ubiquity. When we discuss TV with our friends, people often say, "I just binged X." Does that mean they watched it over a weekend or a month? It's unclear, but demonstrates they dedicated their TV viewing time to the show.

Streaming television apps lend themselves to binge-watching. "Much of this drive has been fueled by Serial TV series and Netflix's pioneering of binge watching with its release of all episodes of a single season at one time."[10] When streaming services drop all episodes for a single season at once, there is nothing to stop viewers from watching the next episode. And since most shows now have elements of serial dramas, we really want to see what happens next. A television serial is "a dramatized action divided into episodes."[11] Most episodes of a serial ends with a cliffhanger, the audience waits in suspense for the next episode. Serials feel like long films that cut in the middle as if waiting for the viewer to binge the next episode or season. By contrast, for a *television series* "the continuity is not of an action but of one or more characters."[12] The television *series* has been the typical form for prime time television genres from detective shows to sitcoms. While the characters' lives extend past a given show, the plot starts anew each episode. Series sometimes introduce serial concepts from multi-part shows to season-ending cliffhangers. However, most episodes remain neatly within themselves. With a series, we can skip episodes without missing much, but for serials, viewers need to see every episode to know of every plot twist. Serials lend themselves to binge-watching because they suck viewers into the plot. We want to know what happens next.

Binge-watching TV shows changes the cultural position of television in our everyday lives. No longer bound by the programming schedule, binge-watching allows us to take entire shows in without interruption. Or we can mix-and-match series. For instance, my wife and I find *The Hand-maid's Tale* to be a very heavy show to binge. Instead, we'll watch one episode a night and pair it with a comedy like *Marvelous Mrs. Maisel* or *Catastrophe*. At the same time we binge-watch a show, streaming allows us to create our own flow.

Since binge-watching is so pervasive, we also have to binge-watch to avoid spoilers. When everyone watches one episode of a show a week, the "water-cooler talk" at the office will revolve around the week's episode. Being part of a workplace or a circle of friends can induce us to watch a specific show, so we can be part of the conversation about that show. We can then keep up with the show, so our colleagues and friends don't spoil the show for us. With binge-watching, this accelerates the whole cycle. Now instead of discussing the latest *episode*, colleagues and friends will discuss the last *season*. If we want to participate in the conversation, we have to try to keep up with those we interact with or risk spoilers. And spoilers are everywhere from Twitter to magazines. For instance, *Rolling Stone* television reviewers provide synopses of entire seasons when a streaming platform releases a show. As a result, binge-watching television becomes a necessary part of the cultural consumption of television.

GOLDEN AGE OF TELEVISION

Television is no longer something we watch as mindless entertainment. For decades, predictable sitcoms and detective dramas ruled the airwaves. As more television stations launched, each station would play the same two or three TV shows 24/7. Since networks no longer relied on reruns during off-season, they started producing cheap-to-produce Reality TV. In the 2000s, television programming was on the way from bad to worse. More and more people were "cutting the cord" as they abandoned cable subscriptions. Then Netflix began streaming full seasons of television shows. These commercial-less shows were easy to sit and watch hour after hour—binge as we now call it. This led television producers to reimagine what is possible on the small screen.

A small group of people makes television programming decisions across the world. These television executives form a tight-knit cultural group who think they know what viewers want to watch. As Timothy Havens explains, "a generation of television professionals worldwide begins to think about television in similar ways, they likewise define for the rest of us the possibilities (and impossibilities) of the medium."[13] As television executives share their perspectives about what works on television, they shape audiences' options. We can only watch shows network executives purchase. When there were fewer channels, this limited our options.

In the "Indians on TV" episode of *Master of None*, Aziz Ansari's character, DV, drives home the point that TV executives make decisions based on a perceived audience. This episode involves fictional television executive Jerry Danvers who refuses to produce a television show with two Indians.

> *Dev: The bigger issue is why can't there be two Indian people in the show?. . .*
>
> *Jerry Danvers: Okay, I'll be frank with you. If I do a show with two Indian guys on the posters, everyone's going to think it's an Indian show. It wouldn't be as relatable to a large mainstream audience.*
>
> *Dev: Yeah, but you would never say that about a show with two white people. Every show has two white people. People don't say that. . .*
>
> *Jerry Danvers: But just to be clear that's not me. Okay, that's the public. Jerry Danvers would love to see two Indian people on a show. Who cares, right? . . . But. . . we're just not at that point.*

Ansari demonstrates through Danvers' character that television executives pass their own biases on to a perceived public. Danvers claims the public is not ready. Because these executives claim to know everything about what people want to watch, it limits the options from which the public has to choose.

As new networks entered the television marketplace, they began to redefine what was possible on television. During the cable era, the explosion of networks turned into the proliferation of limited options. Each cable network plays the same three shows throughout a given day, and most of them are syndicated reruns—"extant films and television programs have been cable's bread and butter."[14] This began to change as streaming services began to act as networks developing their own content. Television streaming platforms did not have to follow the same programming logic of cable and broadcast networks. Whereas the average 30-minute TV show has 7 minutes of commercials and the average 60-minute TV show has 17 minutes of commercials (limiting their shows to 23 minutes and 43 minutes, respectively), streaming platforms have no such requirements. Shows such as *Ozark* regularly stretch over an hour long. Since networks have to cover airtime every night, they create long seasons that run roughly September to April and last at least 22 episodes. Shows produced by streaming platforms often run 6-10 episodes per season. A perennial issue for television producers is finding advertisers. Brands want to associate with television shows that represent their brand, so they too can overdetermine what shows networks produce. However, streaming platforms often do not have commercials in their streaming content (Hulu is one major exception), so they do not answer to advertisers. Finally, streaming platforms have few regulations. Whereas in the United States the Federal Communications Commission (FCC) determines what is appropriate for networks to play over broadcast, there is no parallel body for internet broadcasts. As a result, shows on Netflix, Hulu, and Amazon Prime tend to contain nudity, profanity, and violence.

Then Netflix released two hit dramas in 2013, *House of Cards* and *Orange Is the New Black*. Starring Kevin Spacey, *House of Cards* became the first in a growing list of original series on streaming platforms that starred film actors. In the past, actors tended to make their move from television to film as they grew reputations, but now an increasing number of film actors move to television as television content improves. Another feature of these two Netflix releases was a shortened season with the first season of both shows only 13 episodes long. This is half the length of a standard television drama. It also helps to induce binge-watching because viewers can watch entire seasons in a short period of time. Now streaming platforms regularly produce 6-10 episode seasons. An added feature of these shortened seasons is that 1) it helps to wait for multiple seasons before binge-watching; and 2) it forces viewers to catch-up on last season before watching a new season. While critics argue television content keeps getting better, the culture around television watching keeps changing.

CONCLUSION

When television was first introduced in America, collective consumption was a feature. Often, the first house on the block would host television viewing get-togethers. This made television a social event. The further television sets penetrated society, the more isolating television consumption becomes. First, most homes have a television and there was no need to watch television together. Then, each home bought multiple television sets, so families and roommates no longer had to watch the same programming together. Now, with the ability to stream television programming on any device, people can inhabit the same space as they watch different shows. Whereas television watching existed as a communal and cultural event, today watching TV is an individualized experience. Aside from large and historic events (e.g. the Super Bowl and Barack Obama's inauguration), people rarely watch TV in groups in the same physical location. However, even during the streaming era, there is a tendency for friends, colleagues, and acquaintances to watch the same shows.

When people experience popular culture together, they experience collective effervescence. Collective effervescence occurs when groups of people come together for ritualistic purposes and feel emotional energy from the gathering.[15] Concerts provide a great contemporary example of collective effervescence because when we experience live music with other people, we feel the electricity in the air. Watching television at someone's house can elicit the same type of feelings. As television consumption became more individualized, we lost collective effervescence. However, this does not mean collective effervescence is gone forever. In fact, new communication technologies allow people to watch TV together even if they are not co-located. For instance, many television shows utilize the "two-screen experience" whereby producers entice viewers to participate on a website while they watch a show. Many shows provide Twitter hashtags, so viewers can express their thoughts about an episode with other viewers while the episode airs. Increasingly, television shows, such as *Tiger King*, grow to be must-see-TV events that we experience together, even if not at the same moment.

Social groups are beginning to use streaming technology to connect with one another, far from "bowling alone."[16] Contemporary society does not isolate us, but rather gives us the ability to find people with similar interests who don't live in our local community. People use social media to find people with similar interests and maintain contacts over those networks. Streaming platforms are now nodes of this social interaction. One of the original and strongest forms of digital interaction comes from video games, explored in the next chapter.

NOTES

1. Derek Kompare, *Rerun Nation: How Repeats Invented American Television* (Abingdon: Routledge, 2006), https://doi.org/10.4324/9780203337387.
2. Chuck Tryon, *On-Demand Culture: Digital Delivery and the Future of Movies*, None edition (New Brunswick: Rutgers University Press, 2013).
3. Sut Jhally, *The Codes of Advertising: Fetishism and the Political Economy of Meaning in the Consumer Society* (New York: St. Martin's Press, 1987); Dallas Walker Smythe, "On the Audience Commodity and Its Work," in *Dependency Road: Communications, Capitalism, Consciousness, and Canada*, ed. Dallas Walker Smythe (Norwood: Ablex, 1981), 230-56.
4. Raymond Williams and Ederyn Williams, *Television: Technology and Cultural Form*, Routledge Classics (London; New York: Routledge, 2003), 87, http://www.loc.gov/catdir/toc/fy0708/2003015009.html http://www.loc.gov/catdir/enhancements/fy0701/2003015009-d.html.
5. Smythe, "On the Audience Commodity and Its Work."
6. Jenji Kohan, *Weeds*, television (Lions Gate Television, Tilted Productions, Weeds Productions, 2005).
7. Brian Connor and Long Doan, "Government vs. Corporate Surveillance: Privacy Concerns in the Digital World," in *The Dialectic of Digital Culture*, ed. David Arditi and Jennifer Miller (Lanham: Rowman & Littlefield, 2019), 47-60.
8. Tanya Horeck, Mareike Jenner, and Tina Kendall, "On Binge-Watching: Nine Critical Propositions," *Critical Studies in Television* 13, no. 4 (December 1, 2018): 499-504, https://doi.org/10.1177/1749602018796754.
9. Graeme Turner, "Television Studies, We Need to Talk about 'Binge-Viewing,'" *Television & New Media*, September 26, 2019, 1527476419877041, https://doi.org/10.1177/1527476419877041.

10. Dennis Broe, *Birth of the Binge: Serial TV and the End of Leisure* (Detroit: Wayne State University Press, 2019), 108, http://ebookcentral.proquest.com/lib/utarl/detail.action?docID=5718009.
11. Williams and Williams, *Television: Technology and Cultural Form*, 57.
12. Williams and Williams, 57.
13. Timothy Havens, *Global Television Marketplace* (British Film Institute, 2006), 7.
14. Kompare, *Rerun Nation*, 171.
15. Emile Durkheim, *The Elementary Forms of Religious Life*, ed. Mark S. Cladis, trans. Carol Cosman, 1st ed. (Oxford: Oxford University Press, 2008).
16. Robert D. Putnam, *Bowling Alone: The Collapse and Revival of American Community* (New York: Simon & Schuster, 2000), http://www.loc.gov/catdir/bios/simon054/00027278.html http://www.loc.gov/catdir/description/simon041/00027278.html http://www.loc.gov/catdir/enhancements/fy0705/00027278-t.html http://www.loc.gov/catdir/enhancements/fy0705/00027278-s.html.

6

STREAMING VIDEO GAMES: NEVER OWN A GAME AGAIN

I grew up playing video games. For my birthday in first grade, I received my first video game console: Nintendo Entertainment System (NES). The NES was all the rage and I spent countless hours playing *Super Mario Brothers* and *Duck Hunt*, the two titles included with the system. From the puzzle game *Tetris* to the action-adventure game *The Legend of Zelda*, I played video games far more than I watched television—at least until my family got cable a few years later. When Nintendo released the Super Nintendo Entertainment System (SNES), I once again received it as a birthday present. The enhanced graphics made *Super Mario World* a top choice of mine. But it was the SNES that introduced me to video game football with *Super Play Action Football*. This game started a love affair with football video games that continues for me today. At the same time, I was playing PC-based video games like *Civilization*. All of these games required the purchase of physical game cartridges, floppy-disks, CDs or DVDs and most of them lacked a capacity to play online. However, video games increasingly rely on internet connections to download or stream the game, play with others online, and update software. These digital mechanisms make video games leading platforms of streaming cultural content.

Digital networks have provided platforms for video games since the early Internet. But increased bandwidth enabled an explosion of online gaming. Video games have been fixed to physical software, since their invention. This chapter explores the ways that downloads, and streams have changed the design of video games and the cultures that arise along them. First, I explain how the disintermediation of video games changed the political economy of video games by emphasizing console subscriptions, in-game downloads, and surveillance of personal data. Here we see dramatic changes in the political economy of video games with a new emphasis on free games supported by advertising and in-game purchases. Second, I discuss the ways that online gaming developed its own cultures from esports to in-game friendships. Streaming video games disrupts the monopoly of the console system, but only insofar as it creates new business opportunities for video game companies in the form of unending consumption.

THE CHANGING VIDEO GAME COMMODITY

Unlike other cultural forms, video games developed as a commodity from the start. Initially developed by defense contractor Ralph Baer,[1] the history of video games is the history of selling something. While many programmers spend time tinkering with games, most video games are produced by companies. Early video games were arcade games, which required players to line-up to pump quarters in the machines.

When companies developed the first consoles, they did so under the same logic of the gramophone—sell the machine, but make most of the revenue from selling games to be played on the system. Built into the console system was planned obsolescence because game companies invested heavily in research and development to increase the graphics and computer processing speeds of the consoles.[2] With every new increase in personal computing processing speeds, software developers produced games for the most advanced computers. However, with downloading and streaming games, the political economy of video games evolved from the logic of planned obsolescence to that of unending consumption that relies less on graphics and more on staying connected with a game for years.

The early days of video game development secured a political economy reliant on new systems, new computers, and new games. Each new console system marks an effective arms-race where video game console companies try to imagine what will drive gamers to their systems. For the past two decades the competition has been between Nintendo, Microsoft Xbox and Sony PlayStation. In Jesper Juul's *A Casual Revolution*, Juul describes his experience at the Microsoft keynote at the 2005 Game Developers Conference. While PlayStation and Xbox competed with high-definition (HD) graphics in their new consoles, Nintendo strayed away from HD graphics to focus on the interactive controllers for the Wii.[3] The Wii controller is mimetic – meaning the video game character mimics the actions of the player. The popularity of the Wii led PlayStation and Xbox to develop their own interactive gaming systems that used mimetic controls. Moreover, capitalist competition underpins the development of new generations of video game consoles based on a perceived "consumer." In the current political economy of video games, video game software has become less concerned with high-definition graphics and fast processor speeds, while programmers increasingly focus on hooking players to a game.

Now the focus of video game companies is to monetize every part of a game. Designers no longer think of video game software as a static one-time purchase, but rather as something that can be upgraded, updated, and upstreamed. This means video game development never stops after the game is released. The constant updating of games can be free and beneficial in the case of fixing bugs on one end, but it can be predatory at the other end by locking out features late in the game without paying for more. This is the case for trial video games that tease players into playing a game at no cost only to be forced to pay a fee when they've become hooked. In other cases, the game itself is expandable like *Civilization*. When the initial versions of *Civilization* were released, users purchased the software for a one-time price and could continue playing the game as long as they wanted. However, *Civilization VI* has multiple versions of the game to purchase available on multiple platforms. The base PC version of *Civilization* costs $59.99, and a platinum version costs $119.99. The platinum PC version of the game includes six downloadable content (DLC) packs and two game expansions. This model allows game developers to release the game and continue to release content for players after the game's initial release to earn even more revenue without forcing players to adopt a new game. While the platinum version of *Civilization* includes most expansion packs, early adopters (who are likely dedicated fans) need to purchase the packs as they are released. Now video games are platforms for which game developers can continuously develop and sell to video game players.

Video game companies use streaming technology to create unending consumption through three dominant models: subscriptions, in-game purchases, and surveillance of gamers. These dominant models are not static and often evolve with the games, and most video games incorporate elements of more than one model.

First, subscriptions allow video game companies and video game console companies to make revenue streams constant and predictable. Consider the Xbox, Microsoft developed Xbox Live as a means for gamers to play Xbox games online with friends and random opponents. Xbox Live used to cost $5/month to provide Xbox to access the Internet. This was in addition to your ISP subscription. If you wanted to use an Xbox to access Netflix, you had to pay this fee. The next tier is Xbox Live Gold, which allows subscribers to play games online for $10/month. In addition to playing online Xbox Live Gold includes a couple free games. The top tier is Xbox Game Pass Ultimate for $14.99/month. This includes Xbox Live, over 100 streamed games, and access to exclusive offers. After buying a game, subscribers to Xbox Game Pass Ultimate can access the game from both Xbox and their PC—the function allows players to pick-up wherever they left off on a different system. Nintendo made a subscription even more tempting with NES and SNES emulators included on the Nintendo Switch Online subscription. For $3.99/month or $29.99/year, Nintendo's subscription service allows subscribers to play their favorite 8-bit and 16-bit video games on the Switch along with playing games with friends online and access to exclusive games. However, each profile on a Switch needs its own subscription—Nintendo sells family plans for $39.99/year for up to 8 account holders.

Video game console companies are not the only businesses marketing subscription services. Electronic Arts (EA), one of the biggest video game companies, created a subscription service of its own. EA Access provides subscribers access to a limited number of games in their catalog for unlimited play, a 10% discount on games, and early access to some new titles all for $4.99/month or $29.99/year. Some of EA's biggest titles are yearly sports games like *Madden NFL*, *NHL*, and *NBA Live*, for which EA Access offers the full game of the previous year. On the EA Access FAQ, it lists the following:

> *Is EA Access worth it?*
>
> *We think so! For the cost of a fancy coffee per month or a couple of large pizzas per year you get dozens of games, exclusive early access to new titles and savings on other great EA content. Sounds like a pretty sweet deal. Why not try it out and see what you think?*

Notice the rhetoric here—for a "fancy coffee per month or a couple of large pizzas per year." Any five dollars spent seems like a negligible amount of money in these terms, but when you subscribe to multiple services each month, the money adds up quickly. But just like other subscription services, the question remains: what happens if you stop subscribing? If you buy *Madden NFL 20*,[4] you possess it to play unlimited times, but if you subscribe, you lose it when you unsubscribe. This is just like subscribing to Spotify instead of buying Taylor Swift's *Folklore*. At the same time this meets many players' needs for most games. I'll never forget when I got my Xbox 360—it came free with a laptop purchase—that Christmas, my partner bought four games for me, but I only ever played two of them for more than an hour. For most gamers, the subscriptions to large databases are sufficient to play a number of games at low cost. The subscription approach to game databases also serves gamers who rent video games from video rental stores or Redbox.

While Apple, Google, PlayStation and many more have subscriptions to gaming catalogs, many video games now have or require subscriptions. This is popular among the Massive Multiplayer Online Roleplaying Games (MMORGs).

For instance, *Star Wars: The Old Republic* launched in 2011, gamers can play most of the game for free, but if they want access to all of the expansions, additional levels, DLCs, and added storylines, gamers must subscribe for $14.99/month. Some of the items available in the subscription are available to purchase for $19.99, but the draw is really to subscribe. The biggest subscription MMORG is *World of Warcraft* (*WoW*).[5] In order to play *WoW*, gamers must have a subscription, which costs $14.99/month. Currently, more than 3 million people play every day.[6] When games require a subscription, video game companies increase their revenue exponentially. Instead of spending $50 for a game through a one-time purchase, users can spend more than that amount on a $15/month subscription in 4 months.

Second, in-game purchases provide a mechanism to encourage gamers to continue to spend money on games as long as they play it. This enables video game companies to expand the means of consumption by offering consumption options to players similar to merchandising. Video games can offer gamers anything from new skins to game expansion kits. If a player purchased *Civilization VI* and consistently plays, then it only makes sense for these players to purchase DLCs and expansion packs. This was impossible before video games connected to the Internet. Gamers couldn't play *Super Mario Brothers* on the NES and upgrade his costumes. However, in the streaming era, the consumption of new mods and skins is akin to buying a new wardrobe for each season.

Fortnite[7] is one of the most popular games in the world with 350 million registered accounts. This first-person-shooter by Epic Games quickly attracted a wide player base because it is free-to-play and can be played in three modes (battle royale, survival, and sandbox). While battle royale and survival modes are fairly conventional first-person shooters, the sandbox mode provides a unique tie-in to fans of the popular *Minecraft* video game. By making the connection to other popular video games and providing it free, *Fortnite*'s creators followed a general strategy in popular culture to make blockbuster hits—i.e., do what already works. But how does *Fortnite* make money? Primarily, *Fortnite* earns revenue through in-game purchases of skins.

Video game companies even developed out-of-game purchases that link back into the game. Nintendo created a way for fans to purchase physical toys out-of-game, which then affect the game itself called Amiibo. These toys have near-field-communication (NFC) tags that allow them to communicate with the Switch, Wii U, and Nintendo 3DS. When users purchase an Amiibo, the toy adds elements to the game and stores data in the NFC about game play. This creates an added dimension to unending consumption even though the stream comes from a toy instead of the Internet.

In the case of both subscriptions and in-game purchases, what happens when the game shuts down? Any game "could close down and whilst the app may still exist on an individual's device, many of these games rely on contact with the developer's server to run. If the developer were to cease supporting the game, any items paid for via in-app purchases would suddenly vanish."[8] Similar to the difference between purchasing a CD vs subscribing to a music streaming service, the changing political economy of games moves away from ownership to a license model.[9] This means that no matter how much gamers spend on their games, video games become ephemeral cultural objects that they cannot collect, store or otherwise use without a temporary license.

Third, streaming video games rely on selling private user data obtained through surveillance on networked games. When gaming systems seduce players to subscribe, these companies get the added bonus of monetizing subscriber behavior. Whenever someone with an Xbox Live account plays their Xbox, they stream data back to Microsoft. Of course gamers don't need console subscriptions for console companies to exploit user data. This occurred to me after I bought a Nintendo Switch, but before I subscribed to Nintendo Switch Online. Here is the initial set-up sequence on the Switch:

1. Select Language

2. Select Region

3. End-User License Agreement (must accept)

4. Set-Up Internet Connection

5. Time Zone

6. Option to connect to a TV

7. Set-Up Controllers

8. Select User Icon and Nickname

9. Link to Nintendo Account

10. Parental Controls

This sequence is important for several reasons. First, before you do anything, Nintendo forces users to agree to their terms for the hardware and software. There is no opt-out option. By selecting one's language and region, this sets users up with the correct user agreement. In the End-User License Agreement, Nintendo specifies how it will utilize user information. "We may use and share information that you give to us and information that we collect when you use our products and/or services (including the Console)." In other words, using the Switch entitles Nintendo to use (i.e. sell) user data. Similar to the Xbox, "there is little indication to players what kind of information they are sharing with the videogame or console's producers."[10] While scholars and activists argue for an opt-in instead of an opt-out,[11] Nintendo doesn't even provide an opt-out option. Second, it asks users to connect to the Internet. If a user has no plans to play online, connecting to the Internet would be irrelevant. I blindly connected mine to the Internet without thinking about why I needed to connect it. Nintendo wants users to connect to the Internet because it allows the console company to begin collecting user data. Third, Nintendo wants users to create profiles, so it can more directly correlate data to specific users. Without user profiles, Nintendo has no direct means to discern one user from another. After someone creates a Mii (Nintendo's fun user profiles), Nintendo can begin to individualize user information and correlate some basic gender information. Every time users start a game, Nintendo asks them to log-in as a user. Nintendo collects all of this information in the background.

Just like television, video games profit from selling an audience to advertisers. In the digital era, the use of private user data for advertising may not be obvious. When I turn-on my Switch, I'm not inundated with advertising. Rather, users work to create "profile data, user-generated content and transaction data (browsing behaviour) – a data commodity that is offered for sale by Internet corporations to advertising clients that can select certain user groups they want to target."[12] Nintendo sells these data to other companies that track users with cookies and/or correlate the data to better market to specific demographic groups. In other words, Coca-Cola may be tracking data to see what games a key demographic group plays, then Coca-Cola uses this information to make marketing information—maybe deciding to place a popular video game character on a Coke can. It also leads to product placement in video games, like placing a Coca-Cola cap in *Final Fantasy IV*. But even more insidious is when companies connect social media or Google profiles to game accounts. For instance, gamers can register to play *Fortnite* using their Facebook log-in information (or later connect their Facebook profile to find friends). When users provide *Fortnite* (and its producer Epic Games) with this information, *Fortnite* accesses a trove of data about its players. Video game companies sell user data as an audience commodity to generate revenue and most users are unaware of the hidden processes even though they agree to it.

Streaming technology enables unending consumption for the video game industry. Gamers no longer buy a $50 game cartridge and exit the commodity chain. Now gamers buy a game, subscribe to a service, and buy upgrades in the game all while being surveilled by the video game producer, console company, and myriad other digital intermediaries while they play. At the same time, the culture of playing video games has changed alongside streaming technology.

VIDEO GAME STREAMING CULTURE

Video games emerged from arcade lifestyle. To play most games, players had to be in an arcade and pump coins into the game machine to continue to play. Different rituals arose alongside arcade culture from placing quarters on a machine (to reserve a spot in line) to attracting an audience while a player dominates a game. We can see remnants of these early cultural formations today: quarters have been replaced by in-game purchases and audiences now occur online (I discuss Twitch in the next chapter). Streaming technology creates new opportunities to reimagine gaming culture by reinvigorating old cultural formations through digital networks.

During my freshman year in college, most students in my dorm were obsessed with the first-person shooter *Counter-Strike*.[13] As you walked the halls, there was a constant soundtrack of gunfire, explosions, and yelling as players battled it out. At the time in 2001-2002, campuses were some of the few places with high enough bandwidth for gamers to play the popular game. Many of the players hosted their own servers in my dorm to decrease lag time. However, there was the constant reminder that the players were locally based—for instance, players often yelled across halls instead of using microphones. Fast-forward to 2020, *Counter-Strike* is still an enormously popular game and is one of the dominant games in esports. However, faster broadband allows players to play in the privacy of their home using headphones to talk to other players.

Around the same time, Xbox and PlayStation also developed online multiplayer capabilities. Whereas multiplayer games have a history going back to early arcade games, they required players to be gathered in one place. Several of my friends were big fans of *Halo* (a primarily console-based first-person shooter)[14] and they would have LAN parties where several people would bring Xboxes to someone's place and they would network the Xboxes to allow more than four players. With the release of the second version of *Halo*, gamers could play online and skip the LAN parties by using Xbox Live. Since many video games are more fun to play with friends, online streaming services enabled gamers to play online with friends from home.

However, to play video games online increases unending consumption because everyone playing must have their own version of the video game and subscribe to the console's online service. During COVID-19 social distancing practices, many people took to playing video games with friends online. As a result, new video game practices have arisen. For instance, a group of my friends began playing the Nintendo Switch's

Mario Kart[15] online while chatting on Zoom. *Mario Kart*, like many Nintendo games, provide great party games.[16] Zoom enables them to communicate the same way they would if they were at the same house. While anyone could log-in and watch on Zoom, only those with their own version of the $50 game could play.

Video game culture has headed in two dominant directions as a result of streaming technology. First, streaming enables "casual video games"—games that are "easy to learn to play, fit well with a large number of players and work in many different situation."[17] Second, streaming fosters Massively Multiplayer Online Role-Playing Games (MMORPG)—games that hardcore gamers play with multitudes of others online in virtual worlds. While many games still rely on single-player play at home without online connections, these two directions in video game play have subsequent cultures that arise with them.

Casual games often have low monetary and time investment. As a result, they entice people to play them who otherwise do not think of themselves as "gamers" because they do not require much skill to play ahead of time. They also usually have short sessions, which means there is little time commitment.[18] While these games do not require a lot of time commitment, the short sessions make them even more addicting. Like a well-written fiction novel with short chapters and chapter breaks, the short time commitment to the present task can lure the gamer into playing "just one more" round. Casual games often use the freemium model, which are available for free download, but include options for in-app purchases. In-app purchases on casual games usually help users advance in the game faster than if they played the game. Elizabeth Evans calls this the "monetization of impatience," which as an "economic strategy is ultimately concerned with monetizing a player's impatience and desire to avoid waiting for the game's progression."[19] Players can play free and earn points or in-game currency through extensive play or they can take shortcuts by purchasing items with real-world currency. Evans contends "freemium game economics are not about selling assets or objects but about selling the experience of gameplay, of monetizing the player's ability to control their play and, most significantly, the time and attention they take to play"[20] Many of these games thrive on social media platforms through "connective game platforms" because the games are connected to Facebook, Google or other platforms.[21] These platforms, like *Candy Crush*, sell what David Nieborg calls a "connective commodity" because people want to share their experiences through social media platforms.[22] Games like *FarmVille* become an "extension or appendage to a main platform such as Facebook."[23] Hardcore gamers criticize games like *FarmVille* because they require very little skill to play and amount to a series of options. However, casual video games account for the bulk of video game culture. Streaming culture enables video game players to interact with each other while playing video games.

At the other end of the spectrum are Massively Multiplayer Online games (MMOs). These games require immense skill and players must dedicate inordinate amounts of time. In an MMORPG like *World of Warcraft*, players set-up meetings with their guilds (i.e. teams) to strategize raids (i.e. missions). Notice here that *WoW* has its own lingo, which can be exclusionary to first-timers. However, MMORPGs have a tendency to ensnare players because the worlds are so immersive. I know of two people who dropped out of PhD programs because they spent inordinate amounts of time on *WoW* and could not keep up with studying. MMOs are also creating synergistic opportunities with other aspects of popular culture. Virtual concerts have become popular events in these gaming platforms from U2's *Second Life* concert to DJ Marshmello's

Fortnite show attended by 10 million users.[24] During COVID-19, the live music industry has struggled to find a way to get fans to spend money on live music, but none of their attempts, aside from some network specials, comes close (the Disney Family Sing Along had 10.7 million people tune in live). The rise of virtual concerts demonstrates MMO platforms have a cultural draw unlike other aspects of streaming culture. MMOs create streaming worlds where some gamers spend a large proportion of their lives.

Computer platforms have also developed to distribute games and build community. For instance, Steam is an online platform that labels itself a "community"—note that creators of digital platforms excel in their desire not only to create digital systems, but brand them as communities. Steam sells itself as "the ultimate destination for playing, discussing, and creating games." Games range in cost from free to $60+ and in content from the kitschy *Super Bernie World* (free) to the consecrated *NBA2K20* ($59.99). Steam encourages players to take screenshots and chat with other players in online discussions. It also allows users to access, play, review, and create games for other members of the community. Episode, another computer-based platform, not only gives free games to users, but it provides a simple platform that anyone can use to create their own games. This has become popular with teenage girls who develop games using the platform—similar to choose your own adventure stories.[25] Gaming platforms now invite gamers to participate in broader communities because when people feel like a community, they are more likely to continue logging in—it elicits an effective response from users.

One of the reasons why MMOs and casual games are so seductive for players is the effective responses they elicit. Streaming culture demands attention. Everything relies on a hook. In fact, binge-watching television is an element of wanting more. Video games mastered the effective response.

"Games companies attempt to control and manage effect and the potential emotional states produced by this effect within a particularly narrow bandwidth of possibility."[26] This lends itself to unending consumption because at the point players have an effective response to a game, they want more. Then players can purchase more or subscribe for more money. For instance, *Guitar Hero*[27] and *Rock Band*[28] used in-game purchases to permit players to buy additional songs online. Not only do these mimetic games (games that mirror the player's motions) elicit effective response, the desire to play one's favorite songs draws users to in-game download purchases for more songs.

A critical element to the effective response in video games is the use of achievements.[29] As Alex Dean Cybulski argues, recording high scores has been an integral part of video game culture since the advent of video arcade games. Gamers want to have the high score. As this moved online with Sega's Dreamcast in 1999, gamers could track high scores by connecting with other gamers. Eventually, Microsoft started tracking not only high scores, but created "achievements" that demonstrated every time someone did a specific task. "More often than not these track systems, like achievements on the Xbox 360, cannot be turned off or evaded by opting-out."[30] These pop-up in games in different ways. For instance, *Super Mario Odyssey* allows players to play little matches in the game (like jumping rope or playing volleyball) and compare one's score with others online. These little matches can be quite addicting to see if you can get to the top of the leader board. Yet, these matches have nothing to do with the overall game progression of *Super Mario Odyssey*. Achievements allow gamers to feel connected back into networks of people similar to having one's name as the top score on an arcade machine.

No matter how people prefer to play streaming video games, one thing is certain: streaming video games increases unending consumption. Video games are always already a commodity and the most innovative free games on the Internet are never free. Whether players subscribe to an MMORPG or play a connective platform game on their phone, video game producers devise ways to exploit gamer culture.

CONCLUSION

Streaming culture fundamentally changes the way we interact with video games. We've changed from playing solitary or one-on-one matches in our homes on games that cost around $50 to streaming games with people around the world often for "free." Games only feel free though as three dominant changes to the political economy of video games developed over the past two decades. Video game technology transitioned from planned obsolescence to unending consumption. It used to be the case that new technology drove gamers to buy new consoles and new video games. Now users subscribe, make in-game purchases, and give up their privacy to pay for the use of games. Rather than buying a game and playing it until you beat it, now we move from one game to the next on subscriptions as they come out. *Angry Birds* is addictive until tossing birds into objects becomes boring, then we can move on to *Candy Crush* without ever thinking about *Angry Birds* again. When the games are social, the content of the game doesn't matter as much as whether our friends still play them. Meanwhile, video game producers lurk in the background, monitoring our every interaction with the game. These changes keep us playing and increase the overall revenue for the video game industry.

As the first 100% digital cultural form, video games seemed the perfect place for streaming culture to take root. But alongside video games new cultural practices developed in the streaming era. For instance, Twitch became a popular way for gamers to show off online and watch others play. In the next chapter, I explore emergent cultural forms that arise from streaming technology, such as Twitch.

NOTES

1. Devin C. Griffiths, *Virtual Ascendance: Video Games and the Remaking of Reality* (Lanham: Rowman & Littlefield, 2013).
2. Jesper Juul, *A Casual Revolution: Reinventing Video Games and Their Players*, 1st ed. (Cambridge: The MIT Press, 2012).
3. Juul.
4. John Madden, Sony Interactive Entertainment LLC, and EA Sports (Firm), *Madden NFL 20*, English, 2019.
5. Rob Pardo, Jeff Kaplan, and Tom Chilton, *World of Warcraft*, Microsoft Windows, macOS, Warcraft (Irvine: Blizzard Entertainment, 2004).
6. "Should You Play WoW in 2020? – MMO Population Blog," accessed August 4, 2020, https://mmo-population.com/blog/should-you-play-wow-in-2020/.
7. Epic Games, *Fortnite*, Windows, macOS, Nintendo Switch, PlayStation 4, Xbox One, Xbox Series X, iOS, Android (Cary: Epic Games, Warner Bros. Interactive Entertainment, 2017).
8. Elizabeth Evans, "The Economics of Free: Freemium Games, Branding and the Impatience Economy," *Convergence* 22, no. 6 (December 1, 2016): 575, https://doi.org/10.1177/1354856514567052.
9. Aaron Perzanowski and Jason Schultz, *The End of Ownership: Personal Property in the Digital Economy* (Cambridge: The MIT Press, 2016).
10. Alex Dean Cybulski, "Enclosures at Play: Surveillance in the Code and Culture of Videogames," *Surveillance & Society; Kingston* 12, no. 3 (2014): 431, http://dx.doi.org/10.24908/ss.v12i3.5329.

11. Christian Fuchs, *Social Media: A Critical Introduction* (Thousand Oaks: SAGE Publications Ltd, 2013).
12. Christian Fuchs, "Dallas Smythe Today - The Audience Commodity, the Digital Labour Debate, Marxist Political Economy and Critical Theory. Prolegomena to a Digital Labour Theory of Value," *TripleC: Communication, Capitalism & Critique. Open Access Journal for a Global Sustainable Information Society* 10, no. 2 (September 19, 2012): 708.
13. Minh Le and Jess Cliffe, *Counter-Strike*, Windows, OS X, Linux (Bellevue: Valve, Sierra Studios, 1999).
14. Bungie Studios, *Halo*, Xbox (Bellevue: Xbox Game Studios, 2001).
15. Shigeru Miyamoto, *Mario Kart*, Nintendo (Kyoto, Japan: Nintendo, 1992).
16. Juul, *A Casual Revolution*.
17. Juul, 5.
18. David B. Nieborg, "Crushing Candy: The Free-to-Play Game in Its Connective Commodity Form," *Social Media + Society* 1, no. 2 (July 1, 2015): 2056305115621932, https://doi.org/10.1177/2056305115621932; Evans, "The Economics of Free."
19. Evans, "The Economics of Free," 576.
20. Evans, 575.
21. Nieborg, "Crushing Candy," 1.
22. Nieborg, 2.
23. Benjamin Burroughs, "Facebook and FarmVille: A Digital Ritual Analysis of Social Gaming," *Games and Culture* 9, no. 3 (May 1, 2014): 151-66, https://doi.org/10.1177/1555412014535663.
24. Bijan Stephen, "Fortnite Showed Us the Future of Live Music (and Its Past, Too)," *The Verge*, February 18, 2019, https://www.theverge.com/2019/2/18/18229471/fortnite-marshmello-pleasant-park-live-music-future-past.
25. Jennifer Allen, "How Episode Became the World's Biggest Interactive Fiction Platform," accessed August 7, 2020, https://www.gamasutra.com/view/news/293928/How_Episode_became_the_worlds_biggest_interactive_fiction_platform.php.
26. James Ash, "Attention, Videogames and the Retentional Economies of Affective Amplification," *Theory, Culture & Society* 29, no. 6 (November 1, 2012): 21, https://doi.org/10.1177/0263276412438595.

27. Greg LoPiccolo, Harmonix, and Ryan Lesser, *Guitar Hero*, Nintendo, PlayStation, Xbox (Boston: Harmonix, RedOctane, Activision, Aspyr, 2005).

28. Greg LoPiccolo, Rob Kay, and Dan Teasdale, *Rock Band*, Xbox, PlayStation, Nintendo (Boston: Harmonix, MTV Games, 2007).

29. Ash, "Attention, Videogames and the Retentional Economies of Affective Amplification."

30. Cybulski, "Enclosures at Play," 431.

7

NEW CULTURAL FORMS: DOMINANT, RESIDUAL, AND EMERGENT

As streaming technology develops, people begin to develop new cultural forms. Since COVID-19 trapped everyone at home, people began to develop new ways to use existing streaming technology in unique ways. Six months before I wrote this chapter, people wouldn't have thought about Zoom meetings and Zoom etiquette. Now we're experts and children are learning how to cope with Zoom for virtual schooling. As I type my son is participating in his first week of Kindergarten in an all online environment. His first few days have focused on learning to use streaming technology. At five years old, he now knows how to mute a microphone, provide cues to his teacher that he understands (either with exaggerated expressions or on screen emojis), and use the learning management system for kids, Seesaw. On my computer, I am typing this chapter while I await a Microsoft Teams meeting to introduce a center I run to new graduate students at the University of Texas at Arlington. In my meeting, I can now expect people to use the same basic skills as my five year old learned. For six months, we've seen late night talk show hosts and news shows operate from these same platforms. While I write, we are also in the middle of the 2020 Democratic National Convention, an experiment with digital streaming platforms. We're learning from what we see on television and recreating it in our own everyday lives. Interacting with these streaming services becomes part of our cultural milieu, but how we use them emerges from cultural context.

In this chapter, I introduce Raymond Williams' theory of emergent culture. Williams lays out three types of culture: Dominant, Residual, and Emergent. This triad of cultural forms provides the structure for the rest of the chapter. First, I discuss briefly the dominant forms as illustrated by Netflix, Spotify, and Amazon. Next, I demonstrate how residual forms remain relevant by discussing vinyl records. Finally, I apply this framework to emergent cultural forms: Vloggers and Twitch. Each of these services present new cultural forms that emerged since streaming developed. This chapter helps to conceive of new cultural forms in the streaming era as part of ongoing cultural practices.

STREAMING CULTURE: "DOMINANT, RESIDUAL, AND EMERGENT"

As I discussed in the "Introduction" to this book, culture is the process through which people make symbolic meaning out of everyday things. The focus on the *process* of culture means it is not static, but rather fluid like a stream. Alongside the process of culture, cultures change as well. Therefore, each cultural moment is informed by what came before it. Raymond Williams described this process of cultural change and adaptation through three aspects of culture: dominant, residual, and emergent culture.[1] These are not variations of culture or different time periods, but rather part of the process of cultural change. As new cultural forms develop, the dominant culture appropriates or adapts those aspects into the dominant culture.

First, dominant culture represents the cultural norms within society. Dominant culture is an expression of hegemony—"an inclusive social and cultural formation which indeed to be effective has to extend to and include, indeed to form and be formed from, this whole area of lived experiences."[2] In other words, hegemony is societal power that establishes order and structures our lived reality. Hegemony surrounds us all, and there is no outside. Through hegemonic power, society establishes norms. Within hegemony, a set of practices appears normal to those within a society. Because dominant culture is normal culture, it functions as the everyday life practices for most people and seems almost unobservable. Kind of like when you read a book that expresses your political beliefs, you don't recognize the author wrote the book from a perspective—also known as confirmation bias. Dominant culture fades into the background because of its ubiquity.

Second, residual culture feels like a throwback to a bygone era. But residual cultural forms express opposition to the dominant culture. Residual culture is oppositional primarily because it reminds everyone the dominant culture is not static. Since some people reach to the past and others remain submersed in it, residual culture serves as a reminder that things can be different. When people reach for residual forms, they demonstrate the dominant culture fails to serve the present. Williams claims residual culture "is still active in the cultural process, not only and often not at all as an element of the past, but as an effective element of the present."[3] Residual culture links to the past while calling for a different future.

Third, emergent culture means for Williams "new meanings and values, new practices, new relationships and kinds of relationships are continually being created."[4] Since culture is not static, emergent culture arises to push culture along. However, emergent culture is always fleeting. "To the degree that it emerges, and especially to the degree that it is oppositional rather than alternative, the process of attempted incorporation significantly begins."[5] The process of attempted incorporation is appropriation or cooptation. Over the past few years, much has been written in the popular press about cultural appropriation. This usually occurs when the dominant white culture in the United States steals Black culture. For decades, white people stole Black culture without any reflection. For instance, while white people fawned over Elvis, African Americans continually pointed out that he stole Black culture in the form of music, dance, and style to make rock and roll palatable to racist white people. It wasn't until the 2010s that an increasing number of white people began to see the problems of stealing Black culture. This debate really got going when Miley Cyrus made a video twerking in 2013.[6] The problem lies in the fact that "much incorporation looks like recognition, acknowledgement, and thus a form of *acceptance*."[7] At the same time, it is this incorporation which dulls the sharp point of emergent culture. Appropriation signifies a moment of both respect and death for an emergent culture.

Often, the residual and the emergent express opposition to the dominant cultural order. Through the process of appropriation, the dominant culture eliminates the oppositional tendencies and allows them to function within the dominant order. As a new cultural form emerges it usually does more than offer alternatives, it contains critique of the dominant order. However, as emergent culture becomes more visible, it also loses its oppositional content. Dick Hebdige applied this analysis to the punk subculture in Birmingham, England in the 1970s.[8] When punk originated, working-class youths used it to express opposition to the dominant culture. Punks used engine oil to grease their mohawk haircuts, safety pins to pierce their body, and chains they found in garages as accessories. Fast-forward to the 2000s and punk became decidedly mainstream as part of the dominant culture. Following the popularization of punk aesthetics, mainstream culture uses hair gel to maintain spiked hair and fauxhawks, body piercings can be done at Claire's Boutique in malls, and chain jewelry can be purchased in most stores. Whereas the emergence of punk marked opposition to dominant culture, it now serves as a purely aesthetic aspect of dominant culture.

While these currents of emergence are easy to view through subcultures from punk to hip hop, emergent culture happens everywhere. However, the difficulty with observing emergent culture (especially as an observer ages) is discerning it before it is appropriated. As such, my examples in this chapter suffer always-already from appropriation. Perhaps it would be better to view the emergent forms discussed below as hybrids. Hybrid cultural forms take aspects of various other cultural forms. Here we can see this within streaming media as different forms of media combine using digital technology. By the time the hybrid media become available to the masses, they've already been appropriated by dominant culture.

When I downloaded Napster in 1999, it was at a moment of emergence for the practice of file-sharing. The service was oppositional because it offered everyone with an internet connection the ability to share music—share in the sense that music could be given and taken freely. Napster permitted independent musicians to freely distribute their music and compete for valuable listening time with major acts. By providing a platform for music distribution over the Internet, Napster created a space for opposition to dominant culture.[9] Of course, the file-sharing service became embroiled in lawsuits over whether file-sharing violated copyrights because record labels did not want to provide this space to music fans.[10] Ultimately, Napster's founders were forced to sell the service through bankruptcy negotiations and it was transformed into Rhapsody, the first music subscription service. Napster went from being an emergent cultural form to the dominant form. We can see this process at work with new emergent forms in the uses of streaming technology.

DOMINANT STREAMS

This book has been about the dominant cultural forms in streaming culture. From Apple Music to Xbox Live, these cultural forms express the will of dominant social institutions. The main goal by these streaming platforms is to generate revenue through the commodification of culture. Amazon makes purchasing and renting mainstream films possible through the click of a button while promising unlimited streams of limited content. Spotify provides access through ad-supported or subscription streams to millions of songs, but finding new music outside of the mainstream can be difficult as corporate record labels provide the foundation to all playlists. Nintendo Switch Online provides access to the Nintendo catalog NES and SNES, but Nintendo limits what games can be played on its platforms. Streaming culture is the dominant culture as it provides a platform for unending consumption. That being said, there are further forms that rely on subscriptions and streams of data to exploit economic profit.

Instant Ink

HP started an ink subscription service called "Instant Ink." An Instant Ink subscription uses internet-enabled printers to communicate with HP servers to identify when a printer is low on ink. When the printer notifies HP, the company sends ink in the mail. These subscriptions range from $2.99/month for 50 pages/month to $9.99/month for 300 pages/month. Instant Ink printers stream data about customers' usage habits back to HP, which informs the company when subscribers need refills. These data also ensure HP runs an efficient distribution chain to avoid ink sitting in stores waiting to be purchased. When you purchase a new printer, they tend to come with 1-8 months of "free" ink (in reality the 8-month subscription printers cost more money, so the ink isn't free). However, even to use these services, you must enter credit card information that automatically enrolls you after the prepaid period ends. Free trial periods of most subscription services usually require a credit card number, then the company begins to charge subscribers at the end of the free period—subscribers have to be proactive to cancel subscriptions or they end-up paying for them.

The fascinating aspect of these printers is that HP sells these printers as loss leaders—any product sold below the cost to make it in order to attract customers. The very nice printer I recently purchased for $99 came with a full ink supply, which retails at $75. In other words, the printer's value in the package I purchased was $24. HP knows customers will continue to buy the ink without buying new printers. While I do not know how much ink costs HP to manufacture, it is likely considerably below $75—Costco refills most ink cartridges for under $12. Because ink is so expensive, if anyone is like me, there is not usually a rush to go purchase new ink when the printer runs out. Rather,

I wait until I feel like I need to print something. In fact, when I don't have ink, I don't print. This doesn't benefit HP's business model, which depends on customers running out of ink. By subscribing customers to Instant Ink, HP ensures a consistent unending consumption.

Software, Spyware and Anti-virus

Over the past two decades, software moved online. As a kid, I remember going to software stores with my dad to purchase the newest versions of computer software. Whether it was the newest WordPerfect, Netscape Navigator, or Microsoft Windows, we had to go to a store and purchase physical software on floppy disks and later CDs or DVDs. These boxes contained installation instructions, basic information about the programs (sometimes full user manuals), and warranty information. Until my most recent move, I had a desk drawer filled with this software and paraphernalia. However, as internet connections became faster, more programs went online for updates and later program downloads. But with streaming technology, the emphasis of software companies is now on subscriptions.

Microsoft Office 365 is the quintessential software subscription. The popular suite of office software allows people to write, sort email, create spreadsheets, etc. The original style of Microsoft Office allowed customers to purchase the software and continue using it as long as their machine supported the software. But when Microsoft introduced Office 365 in 2011, it connected users to the software on a yearly (hence 365) subscription model. As long as users continue to subscribe, they can download the newest version of the software. But whenever users stop subscribing, they can no longer use Microsoft Office. Furthermore, a subscription provides subscribers with access to the entire suite in the cloud, so there is no longer a reason to download the suite if a user prefers web applications. Since users can update Office 365 at any time online, physical software is obsolete.

And now, computers don't regularly come equipped with any type of external drive. I recall one desktop I had, which included four external disk drives: 5.25" floppy disk, 3.5" floppy disk, CD-RW, and DVD. As these drives proliferated around 2000, they began to go away as well. By 2000, the 5.25" drive was antiquated and the 3.5" drive was on its last legs, but computer manufacturers kept the 3.5" drive because enough people had old software and files stored on these disks. However, it wasn't long before computers contained only a CD-RW/DVD-RW drive. Around this time, software became available for download and most computer users backed-up their data on USB thumb drives and external hard drives. But by about 2018, few computers contained disk drives and Apple made the move to eliminate USB ports. Computer manufacturers would begin forcing customers to back-up data online (i.e. in the cloud) and download new software.

Antivirus software were some of the first to develop a subscription model. The purchase of Norton's, McAfee's, or Kaspersky's antivirus software provided updates for a limited amount of time—usually one year. The software would continue to work, but without purchasing updates, the software would no longer update for new virus protections—leaving your computer vulnerable to new threats. Over time, antivirus software companies began to limit licenses to one computer—to place them on more computers or devices, customers need to purchase the license for additional devices.

While computer users use antivirus software to protect their devices from viruses, antivirus software often comes as part of security suites that also protect against identity theft. Every new line of computer code creates vulnerabilities for computers, so users must subscribe to block these threats. Ironically, some of the same security companies also provide the keys of entry to potential hackers. In order for hackers to know about vulnerabilities, they need software that directs them to the holes in code. "Spyware vendors frequently use a subscription model, as it allows buyers to minimize risk by parceling out payments over time and terminating payments if a given vulnerability is patched before the subscription expires."[11] Identifying, closing, or exploiting computer vulnerabilities requires constant updates to software, hence the subscription model.

RESIDUAL

How can streaming culture contain residual elements? Here we see pushes against streaming. Whereas streaming culture relies on cultural consumption online without physical media through hyper-individualized consumption (often on mobile devices), residual cultural elements look to past eras where concrete objects exist in a more analog world.

Vinyl

Vinyl record sales dropped precipitously with the mass distribution of compact discs in the 1980s.[12] For over 20 years, vinyl record sales remained below 5 million units per year in the United States.[13] But vinyl sales began to turn around in 2008 around the peak time of iTunes. While music listeners eschewed the CD, they reembraced vinyl, at least in limited circles. One of the reasons vinyl records hung around was because some rock-oriented baby-boomers swore by the "warmth" of vinyl records and hip hop DJs continued to use two turntables and a microphone to remix music. However, something happened with the rise of digital downloads and has accelerated with the move to streaming music as vinyl has experienced a boom.[14]

Vinyl is a residual cultural element because it retains a previous form of cultural consumption. But it also represents opposition to dominant culture today. When CDs arrived in the 1980s, they offered a compact, durable, and high-fidelity medium—vinyl proved inferior. However, with the rise of streaming music, people purchase vinyl records alongside their streaming subscriptions. Music fans did not begin buying CDs. In other words, vinyl buyers want something that is physical and decidedly analog. While streaming kills music ownership, vinyl offers something to collect on big 12″ discs with all of the added artwork and inserts. It turns out some music fans want to own and hold physical analog music.

Even though vinyl is analog, these machines often have electronic hook-ups that allow them to be streamed on Bluetooth speakers and connected to a computer. The fact that these mechanisms provide the connection of analog vinyl to digital devices demonstrates vinyl consumers do not prefer analog consumption, but rather they want the physical object. There has also been a move by some subcultures to produce tape cassettes. Vinyl music as residual culture opposes the dominant cultural consumption of streaming music by providing ownership of a physical commodity.

EMERGENT

People continue to develop new cultural forms that utilize new streaming technologies. Many of these emergent cultural forms develop in opposition to the dominant culture. They exist as cultural hybrids of media consumption and production that did not exist before streaming technology, but rather emerged as sites of resistance. However, as soon as these emergent forms become identifiable to the masses, their oppositional currents tend to have already diminished. In most cases, the following emergent forms already exhibit elements of appropriation by the dominant culture. But their hybrid characteristics and their popularity demonstrate their significance to streaming culture.

Vloggers

In the 15 years since YouTube's launch, the popular video uploading site created one of the first platforms to stream culture. At first, the videos on YouTube provided mainly user-generated content.[15] Over time, the corporate drift of the Google-owned platform has resulted in YouTube becoming the go-to website for music videos, television show excerpts and movies. Now YouTube has a subscription TV service (YouTube TV) that streams live television programs and YouTube originals for $65/month. YouTube also has a streaming music service (YouTube Music Premium) that allows users to download music videos, stream music without ads and listen to music on YouTube when you are multitasking all for $11.99/month. However, these conventional streaming forms pale in comparison to the YouTube phenomenon known as vlogging.

Vlogging is a hybrid media form that plays with the personal commentary of blogs, but they use videos instead of text. Blogs developed in the 1990s as personal websites where bloggers cataloged websites to make the Internet more user-friendly at a time when search engines were lackluster.[16]

Eventually, blogs became a form of commentary about the web addresses they collected. When content management systems (CMS) like Blogger and WordPress developed, these easy-to-use tools allowed anyone with the slightest web-skills to build a website filled with commentary. The most popular blogs combine personal narrative with commentary about a specific subject area. With YouTube, vloggers began providing the same type of content available on blogs, but in video form. Vloggers sometimes reflect on their personal lives or they demonstrate cooking. At other times, they provide comedic entertainment like "HowToBasic."

Vlogs are quintessentially streaming culture. They emerged as commentary on a broken mass-media that did not allow fans to talk back to corporate conglomerates. Jean Burgess and Joshua Green emphasize vlogging's popularity emanates from the opportunity for fans to talk back. "Not only is the vlog technically easy to produce, generally requiring little more than a webcam and basic editing skills, it is a form whose persistent direct address to the viewer inherently invites feedback."[17] Scholars such as Henry Jenkins view this type of feedback as an important part of "convergence culture," which allows consumers to interact with producers.[18] However, as a site of resistance, vlogging has long been appropriated by big corporate media. Many of the most popular vloggers now go by the name "influencer." An influencer is someone with a significant social media following who can leverage that following to make money through advertising. Companies realize that if a vlogger talks about a product on their vlogs, specific demographics see the product placement and do not think of it as crass advertising. Many of these vloggers now try on clothing in shopping "hauls." In these haul videos, someone buys a bunch of products and demos them. These are similar to product profiles in magazines, but without any reflection that the products were sponsored by the manufacturers. In the biggest turn of appropriation, I recently saw a commercial on regular TV where a vlogger discussed Fabletics leggings in the same manner she would her vlog. While many vlogs still pack an independent punch, many are tools of corporate advertising.

Twitch

Video gamers are notorious users of digital technology. Hard core gamers often have jobs as web architects, hackers, and programmers. Gamers created esports (i.e. electronic sports) as a way to take video game playing professional. Esports leagues are competitive spaces that allow gamers to show off their video game skills. Not only do people play these games against each other online, but people fill arenas to watch competitions—my city, Arlington, Texas, has the largest dedicated esports space, which holds 2,500 fans and has different competitions each day of the week. In other words, gamers like to compete, but they also like to watch each other play. Following the rise of esports, it is not surprising that gamers developed a way to broadcast video games for others to watch. This began with the popular webcam streaming service Justin.tv in 2007, which allowed people to tune in to watch other people do all types of mundane things on webcam. Twitch spun-off from Justin.tv in 2011 as a space for gamers to broadcast and communicate with those watching the game.

While gaming has always had a social/watching element among many gamers, Twitch made watching video games a global cultural event. Arcade games were always public spectacles for anyone standing around. Video game consoles forced people to wait turns at someone's house—those waiting became observers. Waiting for one's turn became part of video game culture—my five-year-old son loves watching me play the Switch. Streaming technology allowed video game watching to become mainstream, first with YouTube videos of people playing video games (especially, game walkthroughs), second with Twitch streaming. "Live streaming was allowing gamers of all kinds to *transform their private play into public entertainment.*"[19] The technological mechanisms that facilitate Twitch are quintessentially part of streaming culture.

However, as soon as Twitch launched in 2011, it was already an appropriated site of culture. The early days of video game broadcasts resembled emergent culture. Gamers broadcast their play for enjoyment, and people streamed their play and chatted with them; this was cultural production that was part of capital only to the extent that Justin.tv earned revenue from the activity. But with the launch of Twitch, the oppositional currents of broadcasting oneself and watching others transformed into a money-making machine. According to T.L. Taylor, "By 2017, the site boasted 2.2-plus million unique broadcasters per month with 17,000-plus members in the Twitch Partner Program and 110,000 'creators' in the Affiliates Program—content producers that receive revenue from their streams—and about 10 million daily active users."[20] Twitch runs a website called "Creator Camp" where site operators explain the basics of running streams, and a key component is a page entitled "Get Rewarded." Here potential Twitch creators learn how to monetize their stream. At the same time, these spaces are not policed and could be sites of social and political discussion, but they tend to lack any oppositional aesthetics and many hard core gamers are accused of some of the most egregious racist and sexist language and practices.[21] Twitch stands as a hybrid cultural form that uses streaming technology to connect video games, broadcasting, and chatting, but it does so now within the dominant culture.

CONCLUSION

While streaming culture provides oppositional currents, it becomes quickly appropriated in the interest of the dominant culture. Streaming culture changes so quickly emergent cultural forms become appropriated by the dominant culture before most people know they exist. This demonstrates the fleeting nature of streaming culture. With previous media, a change to distribution medium would take some time for infrastructure to change. When the CD developed, it took time for people to purchase CD players to replace their record players. This is not the case for streaming culture. When a new app develops, users download it (often for free) and begin making new meanings with the app. Those meanings develop and circulate online among streaming cultures who then make the app and its usage ubiquitous.

The emergent forms of streaming culture could be seen as disruptive. But as I discussed in Chapter 2, disruption generally means a change in business models, not a revolutionary break. This is vivid in Amazon's purchase of Twitch in 2014 for $970 million.[22] Whereas Twitch users disrupted media consumption, they did so only to change the site of media consumption. Amazon showed its media power by purchasing the three-year-old service for far less than its value six years later. No one would argue that streaming video games is a revolutionary act, but the fact that it sold for so much in such a short time demonstrates Twitch is situated within the dominant culture (otherwise it wouldn't be worth so much). Streaming culture changes so fast oppositional cultural forms get appropriated before they can reach their full potential.

NOTES

1. Raymond Williams, *Marxism and Literature*, Marxist Introductions (New York: Oxford University Press, 1977).
2. Williams, 111.
3. Raymond Williams, "Moving from High Culture to Ordinary Culture," in *Convictions*, ed. N. McKenzie (London: MacGibbon & Kee, 1958), 122.
4. Williams, 123.
5. Williams, 124.
6. Dodai Stewart, "On Miley Cyrus, Ratchet Culture and Accessorizing With Black People," *Jezebel*, June 20, 2013, https://jezebel.com/on-miley-cyrus-ratchet-culture-and-accessorizing-with-514381016.
7. Williams, "Moving from High Culture to Ordinary Culture," 124-25.
8. Dick Hebdige, *Subculture, the Meaning of Style* (London: Methuen, 1979).
9. David Arditi, *ITake-Over: The Recording Industry in the Streaming Era*, 2nd ed. (Lanham: Lexington Books, 2020).
10. David Arditi, *Criminalizing Independent Music: The Recording Industry Association of America's Advancement of Dominant Ideology* (Saarbrücken: VDM Verlag, 2007).
11. Patrick Burkart and Tom McCourt, *Why Hackers Win: Power and Disruption in the Network Society*, 1st ed. (Oakland: University of California Press, 2019), 80.
12. Arditi, *ITake-Over*.
13. According to the yearly the *Recording Industry in Numbers* report published yearly by the International Phonographic Industry (IFPI).
14. Michael Palm, "Analog Backlog: Pressing Records during the Vinyl Revival," *Journal of Popular Music Studies* 29, no. 4 (December 1, 2017): n/a-n/a, https://doi.org/10.1111/jpms.12247; Michael Palm, "The New Old: Vinyl Records after the Internet," in *The Dialectic of Digital Culture*, ed. David Arditi and Jennifer Miller (Lanham: Lexington Books, 2019), 149-62.
15. Jean Burgess and Joshua Green, *YouTube: Online Video and Participatory Culture*, 1st ed. (Cambridge; Malden: Polity, 2009).

16. Rebecca Blood, *We've Got Blog: How Weblogs Are Changing Our Culture* (New York: Basic Books, 2002).
17. Burgess and Green, *YouTube*, 54.
18. Henry Jenkins, *Convergence Culture: Where Old and New Media Collide* (New York: New York University Press, 2006).
19. T. L. Taylor, *Watch Me Play: Twitch and the Rise of Game Live Streaming* (Princeton; Oxford: Princeton University Press, 2018), 6.
20. Taylor, 3.
21. Noah Smith, "Racism, Misogyny, Death Threats: Why Can't the Booming Video-Game Industry Curb Toxicity?," *Washington Post*, February 26, 2019, https://www.washington post.com/technology/2019/02/26/racism-misogyny-death-threats-why-cant-booming-video-game-industry-curb-toxicity/.
22. German Lopez, "Why Amazon Spent $970 Million to Buy Twitch," *Vox*, August 26, 2014, https://www.vox.com/2014/8/26/6067085/amazon-twitch-tv-video-games-live-streaming-league-of-legends-dota-2.

8

CONCLUSION

On July 31, 2020, President Donald Trump announced he would consider banning TikTok from the United States if a American company couldn't buy it.[1] TikTok is a video app that started as a way for users to share short videos, usually lip-synching to popular music. Founded as Musical.ly in 2014, Chinese company ByteDance purchased the app and merged it with their own app TikTok in 2017. The app's primary user base is teenagers who have become quite adept at participating in memes and "challenges" using TikTok's user-friendly interface. TikTok remained under most adult Americans' radar until Trump's infamous Tulsa, Oklahoma rally where about 6,200 people showed up to a 20,000 person arena for a Trump rally. TikTok users created videos in which they "accidentally" reserved two tickets to the rally but remember they can't make it because they have to do outlandish things like "walk my fish" instead. This meme led the Trump Campaign to believe exponentially more people reserved tickets than the capacity of the arena. Much to

Trump's surprise, his fans sparsely attended the COVID-era rally.[2] Many commentators believe the President's actions to shut-down TikTok because it was a Chinese-owned "security threat" stemmed from the TikTok users' call-to-action.[3] While the political outcome of TikTok users' attempt to buy all of the Tulsa rally tickets is debatable, streaming culture facilitated comedic collective action.

While TikTok appears to present emergent culture that resists the dominant culture, it's difficult to say how far this resistance goes for sustained organization and collective action. Will these TikTokers go on to disrupt politics? Or was this equivalent to a prank phone call? It will take time to tell, but it is likely to be over-hyped like the "Twitter revolutions" of 2009-2011. As with all technology, social media is a tool that can be used in different ways. To imagine technology "does" anything is technological determinism. Technological determinism is the belief that technology fundamentally alters the social fabric—it does this on its own and people merely do what technology allows. However, it is people who create and deploy technologies for specific purposes. We see technological determinism in the idea that TikTok "does" anything other than provide people with the ability to do things. Furthermore, TikTok took a dark turn when users began posting videos about being Holocaust survivors.[4] All of a sudden, the streaming video site looked a lot more like other social media websites that have become breeding grounds for disinformation, conspiracy theories and right-wing fascists.[5] TikTok, like all social media and streaming technologies, can only do what people do with it. Unfortunately, the ubiquity of TikTok makes it only as strong as its weakest link.

Streaming cultural content is now the dominant form of cultural consumption as demonstrated by the explosion of services like Netflix, Spotify, TikTok and Hulu. This marks a shift from collecting material cultural content to accessing it. In the process, cultural norms about consumption have been upended. We have access to seemingly limitless amounts of cultural content, but our access is dependent on any given service's willingness and ability to license the content. Whereas consumption was once finite, it is now unending. As a result, the divisions we construct around different media become less important because it all becomes available through the stream in our homes and on our devices. TikTok streams represent the quintessential blurring between types of media. A typical short video involves someone lip syncing to a popular song to comedic effect and they can be easily shared via social media.

This book demonstrated how our streaming cultures operate alongside streaming technology that streams culture. These technologies can only do what they are programmed to do. In capitalist society, they are programmed to generate revenue. From Apple TV to *World of Warcraft*, the bottom line isn't about the culture they stream, but how much revenue and profit they create. A system focused on creating as much profit from cultural commodities as possible uses streaming technology to support unending consumption.

SUBSCRIPTIONS AND UNENDING CONSUMPTION

Today subscriptions are everywhere as corporations attempt to expand the means of consumption in what I describe as unending consumption. While subscriptions rely on streams of data, they did not and do not always rely on streaming technology. The printed word offered the first subscriptions in the form of book, newspaper and magazine subscriptions. Newspapers and magazines thrived on this business model as their regular printing intervals (hence the term periodicals) ensured that subscribers received the current issue.

Subscriptions moved from the printed word to other media. For example, Columbia House was a subscription service that would mail music to subscribers on a monthly basis. I first signed up for this service in middle school. They enticed subscribers with 12 CDs for $1. After the initial batch of CDs, subscribers would receive two CDs in the mail each month. However, if you didn't want the CD, you needed to ship it back or pay the full price of the CDs. After receiving my free CDs, I stopped the subscription, but I had a friend who ended up owing the company $150. Subscriptions moved into other areas from coffee and cheese to toys and underwear. The model works because people subscribe and maintain their automatic subscriptions. Media companies use streaming technology to advance subscriptions because it ensures constant and consistent cash flows. At the same time, it creates unending consumption—the acceleration of the expansion of the means of consumption.

As I described in Chapter 1, unending consumption is a logical phase of capitalism. Capitalism is an economic system that relies on the endless accumulation of capital using a wage labor system. Throughout capitalism there have been cyclical moments when an oversupply of goods caused the whole system to crash. Capitalists have tried to figure out ways to avoid these crashes. The number one problem is when a market becomes saturated—those people who can afford to purchase a good already own it. Industrial capitalism attempted to fix the problem by bringing more people into the system: more people able to buy a good means more goods to sell. This was part of Henry Ford's logic in what became known as Fordism—pay workers enough for them to buy a Ford vehicle. But again, as the logic of Fordist capitalism reached its limits, capitalists discovered the best way to solve the crises of capitalism was to expand the means of consumption—making it possible for consumers to buy more goods. One of the primary mechanisms the expansion of the means of consumption works through is planned obsolescence, especially of cultural goods. A person only needs one record player, but they will buy as many records as they have cash to buy them. Later, capitalism made it so we no longer even needed the cash to buy the records because we charge them to credit cards through burgeoning personal credit card debt.

With the expansion of the means of consumption, capitalism became so super charged that the goods we consumed never even got used. Fast capitalism[6] is the moment when text, film, and music became so ubiquitous that we couldn't keep pace to read, watch or listen to the texts produced. In other words, if we can't listen to all of the music produced in a single year, there is clearly overproduction. People would even buy more music than they cared to listen to. How do capitalists handle the situation? They changed the model. After selling $0.99 downloads of songs, for instance, record labels discovered there was leftover value in consumption. Instead of buying $45 worth of CDs or vinyl records each year, they may only buy $20 worth of downloads. Labels recognized consumers had $25 of value to be used in some other way. So they developed streaming subscriptions for roughly $10/month or $120/year. But the value doesn't stop at subscriptions, labels hope their consumers will also purchase vinyl, listen to radio, and buy band merchandise. This is unending consumption.

CAUGHT IN THE STREAM

Because a stream remains in constant motion, it is difficult to describe any given streaming app. Where software used to contain version numbers, streaming applications are a constant work in progress. Often times, I notice a change to a user interface before a bigger announced change happens. But that is streaming culture—an ever-moving process of symbolic meaning making. Over long periods of time, we can see the changes, but as they pass it can be difficult to distinguish the differences. These subtle changes made by corporate executives bring us along for the ride as we feel like our needs are being fulfilled. Unfortunately, our needs become one-dimensional as our existence becomes a pursuit of commodity consumption.[7]

With the streaming wars, different streaming companies vie for our subscriptions. Each new subscription tempts us. They tempt us with ease of use, better technology, a central point for content, but they never fulfill our needs. During COVID-19, my wife and I creep towards the proverbial end of the Internet—what I mean is we've come to the end of what we care to watch. With so many television shows on production pause, we've binge-watched ever more series—and we have a lot of extra time to watch television because of the pandemic. Yet we keep finding the shows we want to watch require new subscriptions. We debate about whether or not subscribing to HBO Max or Showtime will satiate our television binge appetite. The explosion of new streaming services means evermore services to subscribe to. When does it end?

Some predict we will eventually have the Walmart of subscription services where we subscribe to one service to access all media. In my estimation, this will not happen. The prediction harkens back to the heyday of cable subscriptions when monopoly capitalism ruled. There is a case to be made that Amazon acts in monopolistic ways, but as far as streaming culture, it is one of many players. The problem has to do with the licensing of content. As long as a company, especially a TV network or film studio, feels they can earn enough revenue from a streaming service that licenses their own content, they will create the service.

Subscribing to the right number of services becomes increasingly difficult within streaming culture. If your friends and colleagues regularly discuss a TV show that airs on HBO Max, then there is social pressure to subscribe as well. The collective pressure of fitting in and being part of a community encourages us to subscribe to more services. But being a savvy consumer can mean being socially left out of your friend group. After all, culture is the process through which we make symbolic meaning out of signs, so being left out means not understanding the world around you in your everyday life. For instance, when everyone started making Joe Exotic references at the beginning of the pandemic, I was mostly clueless. For instance, hearing someone call someone a "Carole Baskin" meant nothing to me, until I streamed some of *Tiger King*—then everything made sense. However, I do not feel like watching *Tiger King* made me a better person, fulfilled some deep need, or led to any polit-ical action; rather, it was a mildly entertaining way to waste a few nights while I was locked in due to COVID-19. The compulsion to subscribe to new streams may make us closer with our friends, but the subscriptions themselves are rarely fulfilling.

STREAMING IN THE FUTURE

The theme of this book traces a new phase of capitalism, unending consumption, by pointing to the logic of earlier phases. For me, unending consumption feels like a telos, an end. But I'm not naïve enough to think there is an end to phases of capitalism. As with emergent forms of culture, new forms of capitalism are hard to view when you are caught in the dominant form. In many dystopian visions of the future, one corporation controls everything we consume. While Amazon often feels like this type of goliath, there is no reason to think it will own everything because it can't even control streaming licenses.

In fact, as corporations grow larger, there is often a parallel growth in craft-based capitalism. At the same time InBev, the world's largest beer company, buys more and more breweries, there is an explosion of craft breweries in cities and towns across America, and many of these small breweries don't even distribute their products. While Amazon grew exponentially larger as a retail behemoth, Etsy developed as a way to distribute craft homemade goods. Towns across America are revitalizing their downtowns with small businesses at the same time department stores in malls close. We can place independent cultural content on the Internet at the same time that content is crowded out by bigger corporate content creators. People find ways around corporate gatekeepers and corporate gatekeepers find ways to incorporate independent producers, but the process continues.

Perhaps the step beyond unending consumption is a realm of nonprofit consumption. Small community creators coming together to produce cultural goods using streaming technology to distribute their content. Or maybe a new regime of privacy laws disallows corporate data tracking, taking a leg out of unending consumption, and forcing corporations to rethink the way they generate revenue. Or perhaps global climate change hits a tipping point that forces us to unplug our digital technology and focus on local community cultural creation.

Regardless of what comes after unending consumption, the logic of unending consumption will create its own undoing. People will hit a point where they don't want to subscribe to more services. Since culture is ever-changing, we can't expect streaming culture to remain a dominant form. Music, movies, television and video games will continue to blur, but will mainly remain in their discrete spheres. While streaming culture transforms the way we consume culture and the fundamental structure of capitalism, the moving nature of both streaming and culture points to an eminent shift in the structure of society.

NOTES

1. Jason Wells and Megha Rajagopalan, "Trump Said He Plans To Ban TikTok From The US," *BuzzFeed News*, July 31, 2020, https://www.buzzfeednews.com/article/jasonwells/trump-plans-ban-tiktok-us.

2. Peter Wade, "Racism, Lies, and Empty Seats: The Embarrassment That Was Trump's Rally," *Rolling Stone*, June 21, 2020, https://www.rollingstone.com/politics/politics-news/racism-lies-empty-seats-the-embarrassment-that-was-trump-rally-1018329/; Taylor Lorenz, Kellen Browning, and Sheera Frenkel, "TikTok Teens and K-Pop Stans Say They Sank Trump Rally," *The New York Times*, June 21, 2020, sec. Style, https://www.nytimes.com/2020/06/21/style/tik-tok-trump-rally-tulsa.html; William Goldschlag, "Trump's Rally, Rally Embarrassing Night in Tulsa," *Newsday*, June 22, 2020, https://www.newsday.com/long-island/politics/bolton-book-trump-health-rally-tulsa-coronavirus-biden-conventions-barr-berman-1.45969100.

3. Abram Brown, "Is This The Real Reason Why Trump Wants To Ban TikTok?," *Forbes*, August 1, 2020, https://www.forbes.com/sites/abrambrown/2020/08/01/is-this-the-real-reason-why-trump-wants-to-ban-tiktok/.

4. Jack Guy, "TikTok Holocaust Trend 'hurtful and Offensive,' Says Auschwitz Museum," *CNN*, August 27, 2020, https://www.cnn.com/2020/08/27/tech/auschwitz-tiktok-trend-scli-intl/index.html.

5. Mark Andrejevic, *Infoglut: How Too Much Information Is Changing the Way We Think and Know*, 1st ed. (New York: Routledge, 2013); David Arditi and Jennifer Miller, eds., *The Dialectic of Digital Culture* (Lanham: Lexington Books, 2019).

6.   Ben Agger, *Fast Capitalism* (Urbana: University of Illinois Press, 1988).

7.   Herbert Marcuse, *One-Dimensional Man: Studies in the Ideology of Advanced Industrial Society* (Boston: Beacon Press, 1991).

BIBLIOGRAPHY

2002 DirecTV DSL "End of the Internet" Commercial. Accessed March 5, 2020. https://www.youtube.com/watch?v=_uXtWIg_A7M.

Adorno, Theodor W. "The Form of the Phonograph Record." In *Essays on Music/Theodor W. Adorno*, edited by Theodor W. Adorno, Richard D. Leppert, and Susan H. Gillespie, 277–80. Berkeley: University of California Press, 2002.

Agger, Ben. *Fast Capitalism*. Urbana: University of Illinois Press, 1988.

Agger, Ben. *Speeding Up Fast Capitalism: Cultures, Jobs, Families, Schools, Bodies*. Boulder: Routledge, 2004.

Agger, Ben. *Oversharing: Presentations of Self in the Internet Age*. New York: Routledge, 2011.

Aglietta, Michel. *A Theory of Capitalist Regulation: The US Experience*. Translated by David Fernbach. New edition. New York: Verso, 2001.

Allen, Jennifer. "How Episode Became the World's Biggest Interactive Fiction Platform." Accessed August 7, 2020. https://www.gamasutra.com/view/news/293928/How_Episode_became_the_worlds_biggest_interactive_fiction_platform.php.

Andrejevic, Mark. *Infoglut: How Too Much Information Is Changing the Way We Think and Know*. 1st ed. New York: Routledge, 2013.

Arditi, David. "Billboard Plays Catch-up to YouTube's Dominance." *The Tennessean*. March 9, 2020, Online edition, sec. Opinion. https://www.tennessean.com/story/opinion/2020/03/09/billboard-catches-up-to-youtube-dominance/5005889002/.

Arditi, David. Criminalizing Independent Music: The Recording Industry Association of America's Advancement of Dominant Ideology. *VDM Verlag*, 2007.

Arditi, David. "Downloading Is Killing Music: The Recording Industry's Piracy Panic Narrative." Edited by Victor Sarafian and Rosemary Findley. *Civilisations, The State of the Music Industry*, 63, no. 1 (July 2014): 13–32.

Arditi, David. *ITake-Over: The Recording Industry in the Digital Era*. Lanham: Rowman & Littlefield Publishers, 2014.

Arditi, David. "Digital Subscriptions: The Unending Consumption of Music in the Digital Era." In Annual Meeting of the American Sociological Association. Seattle, 2016.

Arditi, David. "Digital Subscriptions: The Unending Consumption of Music in the Digital Era." *Popular Music and Society* 41, no. 3 (2018): 302–18. https://doi.org/10.1080/03007766.2016.1264101.

Arditi, David. "Digital Hegemony: Net Neutrality, the Value Gap, and Corporate Interests." In *The Dialectic of Digital Culture*, edited by David Arditi and Jennifer Miller, 13–28. Lanham: Lexington Books, 2019.

Arditi, David. *ITake-Over: The Recording Industry in the Streaming Era*. 2nd ed. Lanham: Lexington Books, 2020.

Arditi, David, and Jennifer Miller, eds. *The Dialectic of Digital Culture*. Lanham: Lexington Books, 2019.

Ash, James. "Attention, Videogames and the Retentional Economies of Affective Amplification." *Theory, Culture & Society* 29, no. 6 (November 1, 2012): 3–26. https://doi.org/10.1177/0263276412438595.

Berkowitz, Joe. "Watching Movies with Friends on Zoom or Google Hangouts Can Make Quarantine Less Dreary." *Fast Company*, March 20, 2020. https://www.fastcompany.com/90479962/watching-movies-with-friends-on-zoom-or-google-hangouts-can-make-quarantine-less-dreary.

Blake, Emily. "Services like YouTube Largely Blamed for the Music 'value Gap' in New Report." *Digital News*. April 12, 2016. http://mashable.com/2016/04/12/music-value-gap/.

Blood, Rebecca. *We've Got Blog: How Weblogs Are Changing Our Culture*. New York: Basic Books, 2002.

Böttger, Timm, Felix Cuadrado, Gareth Tyson, Ignacio Castro, and Steve Uhlig. "Open Connect Everywhere: A Glimpse at the Internet Ecosystem through the Lens of the Netflix CDN." ArXiv:1606.05519 [Cs], June 17, 2016. http://arxiv.org/abs/1606.05519.

Bourdieu, Pierre. *Distinction: A Social Critique of the Judgement of Taste*. Cambridge: Harvard University Press, 1984.

Bower, Joseph L., and Clayton M. Christensen. "Disruptive Technologies: Catching the Wave." *Harvard Business Review*, January 1, 1995. https://hbr.org/1995/01/disruptive-technologies-catching-the-wave.

Broe, Dennis. *Birth of the Binge: Serial TV and the End of Leisure*. Detroit: OnixTransformation. OnixModel. CityOfPublication; Wayne State University Press, 2019. http://ebookcentral.proquest.com/lib/utarl/detail.action?docID=5718009.

Brown, Abram. "Is This The Real Reason Why Trump Wants To Ban TikTok?" *Forbes*, August 1, 2020. https://www.forbes.com/sites/abrambrown/2020/08/01/is-this-the-real-reason-why-trump-wants-to-ban-tiktok/.

Bungie Studios. Halo. Xbox. Halo. Bellevue: Xbox Game Studios, 2001.

Burgess, Jean, and Joshua Green. *YouTube: Online Video and Participatory Culture*. 1st ed. Cambridge; Malden: Polity, 2009.

Burgess, Jean, Joshua Green, Henry Jenkins, and John Hartley. *YouTube: Online Video and Participatory Culture*. 1st ed. Cambridge; Malden: Polity, 2009.

Burkart, Patrick, and Tom McCourt. *Digital Music Wars: Ownership and Control of the Celestial Jukebox*. New York: Rowman & Littlefield Publishers, 2006.

Burkart, Patrick, and Tom McCourt. *Why Hackers Win: Power and Disruption in the Network Society*. 1st ed. Oakland: University of California Press, 2019.

Burroughs, Benjamin. "Facebook and FarmVille: A Digital Ritual Analysis of Social Gaming." *Games and Culture 9*, no. 3 (May 1, 2014): 151–66. https://doi.org/10.1177/1555412014535663.

Caramanica, Jon. "The Rowdy World of Rap's New Underground." *The New York Times*, June 22, 2017, sec. Arts. https://www.nytimes.com/2017/06/22/arts/music/soundcloud-rap-lil-pump-smokepurrp-xxxtentacion.html.

Cohen, Stanley. *Folk Devils and Moral Panics: The Creation of the Mods and Rockers*. New York: Routledge, 2011. http://public.eblib.com/EBLPublic/PublicView.do?ptiID=684015.

Connor, Brian, and Long Doan. "Government vs. Corporate Surveillance: Privacy Concerns in the Digital World." In *The Dialectic of Digital Culture*, edited by David Arditi and Jennifer Miller, 47–60. Rowman & Littlefield, 2019.

Cybulski, Alex Dean. "Enclosures at Play: Surveillance in the Code and Culture of Videogames." *Surveillance & Society* 12, no. 3 (2014): 427–32. http://dx.doi.org/10.24908/ss.v12i3.5329.

Dean, Jodi. *Blog Theory: Feedback and Capture in the Circuits of Drive*. 1st ed. Malden, MA: Polity, 2013.

Dick, Kirby. This Film Is Not Yet Rated. *Documentary. Independent Film Channel (IFC), Netflix, British Broadcasting Corporation (BBC)*, 2006.

Durkheim, Emile. *The Elementary Forms of Religious Life*. edited by Mark S. Cladis. Translated by Carol Cosman. 1st ed. Oxford: Oxford University Press, 2008.

Epic Games. *Fortnite*. Windows, macOS, Nintendo Switch, PlayStation 4, Xbox One, Xbox Series X, iOS, Android. Cary: Epic Games, Warner Bros. Interactive Entertainment, 2017.

Evans, Elizabeth. "The Economics of Free: Freemium Games, Branding and the Impatience Economy." *Convergence* 22, no. 6 (December 1, 2016): 563–80. https://doi.org/10.1177/1354856514567052.

Fuchs, Christian. "Dallas Smythe Today - The Audience Commodity, the Digital Labour Debate, Marxist Political Economy and Critical Theory. Prolegomena to a Digital Labour Theory of Value." *TripleC: Communication, Capitalism & Critique. Open Access Journal for a Global Sustainable Information Society* 10, no. 2 (September 19, 2012): 692-740.

Fuchs, Christian. *Social Media: A Critical Introduction.* Thousand Oaks: SAGE, 2013.

Fuchs, Christian. "Hearing the Contradictions: Aesthetic Experience, Music and Digitization." *Cultural Sociology* 12, no. 3 (July 13, 2018): 289–302. https://doi.org/10.1177/1749975518776517.

Gay, Paul du, Stuart Hall, Linda Janes, Hugh McKay, and Keith Negus. *Doing Cultural Studies: The Story of the Sony Walkman.* 2nd ed. Los Angeles: SAGE, 2013.

Gillespie, Tarleton. *Wired Shut: Copyright and the Shape of Digital Culture.* Cambridge: MIT Press, 2007.

Goldschlag, William. "Trump's Rally, Rally Embarrassing Night in Tulsa." *Newsday*, June 22, 2020. https://www.newsday.com/long-island/politics/bolton-book-trump-health-rally-tulsa-coronavirus-biden-conventions-barr-berman-1.45969100.

Grazian David. *Mix It Up: Popular Culture, Mass Media, and Society.* 2nd ed. New York: W.W. Norton, Incorporated, 2017.

Griffiths, Devin C. *Virtual Ascendance: Video Games and the Remaking of Reality.* Lanham: Rowman & Littlefield, 2013.

Guy, Jack. "TikTok Holocaust Trend 'hurtful and Offensive,' Says Auschwitz Museum." *CNN*, August 27, 2020. https://www.cnn.com/2020/08/27/tech/auschwitz-tiktok-trend-scli-intl/index.html.

Hall, Stuart. "Encoding, Decoding." In *The Cultural Studies Reader*, edited by Simon During, 3rd ed, xii, 564 p. London; New York: Routledge, 2007. http://www.loc.gov/catdir/toc/fy0906/2009286081.html.

Hall, Stuart, Jessica Evans, and Sean Nixon, eds. *Representation*. 2nd ed. London: SAGE; The Open University, 2013.

Hanrahan, Nancy Weiss. "Digitized Music and the Aesthetic Experience of Difference." In *The Dialectic of Digital Culture*, edited by David Arditi and Jennifer Miller, 165–79. Lanham: Lexington Books, 2019.

Havens, Timothy. Global Television Marketplace. *British Film Institute*, 2006.

Hebdige, Dick. *Subculture, the Meaning of Style*. London: Methuen, 1979.

Hesmondhalgh, David, Ellis Jones, and Andreas Rauh. "SoundCloud and Bandcamp as Alternative Music Platforms." *Social Media + Society* 5, no. 4 (October 1, 2019): 2056305119883429. https://doi.org/10.1177/2056305119883429.

Horeck, Tanya, Mareike Jenner, and Tina Kendall. "On Binge-Watching: Nine Critical Propositions." *Critical Studies in Television* 13, no. 4 (December 1, 2018): 499–504. https://doi.org/10.1177/1749602018796754.

Horkheimer, Max, and Theodor W. Adorno. "The Culture Industry: Enlightenment as Mass Deception." In *Dialectic of Enlightenment*, xvii, 258 p. New York: Herder and Herder, 1972.

Hornaday, Ann. "What Is a Movie? With Theaters Shuttering, the Question Gets Real." *Washington Post*, March 19, 2020, sec. Perspective. https://www.washingtonpost.com/entertainment/what-is-a-movie-with-theaters-shuttering-the-question-gets-real/2020/03/18/930f16ec-6874-11ea-9923-57073adce27c_story.html.

Jenkins, Henry. *Convergence Culture: Where Old and New Media Collide.* New York: New York University Press, 2006.

Jhally, Sut. *The Codes of Advertising: Fetishism and the Political Economy of Meaning in the Consumer Society.* New York: St. Martin's Press, 1987.

Juul, Jesper. *A Casual Revolution: Reinventing Video Games and Their Players.* 1st ed. Cambridge: The MIT Press, 2012.

Kittler, Friedrich A. *Gramophone, Film, Typewriter.* Stanford: Stanford University Press, 1999.

Kohan, Jenji. Weeds. Television. Lions Gate Television, Tilted Productions, Weeds Productions, 2005.

Kompare, Derek. *Rerun Nation: How Repeats Invented American Television.* Abingdon: Routledge, 2006. https://doi.org/10.4324/9780203337387.

Lang, Brent. "Viola Davis Knows What's Wrong With Hollywood… and How to Fix It." *Variety (blog)*, September 4, 2018. https://variety.com/2018/film/features/viola-davis-widows-pay-gap-hollywood-1202924041/.

Lauria, Peter. "Universal Has A Big Stake In Beats That's Worth Nearly $500 Million." *BuzzFeed*, May 8, 2014, sec. Business. http://www.buzzfeed.com/peterlauria/universal-music-will-make-nearly-500-million-on-apples-beats.

Le, Minh, and Jess Cliffe. *Counter-Strike.* Windows, OS X, Linux. Bellevue: Valve, Sierra Studios, 1999.

Levitan, Steven, and Christopher Lloyd. Modern Family. Comedy, Drama, Romance. Levitan/Lloyd, 20th Century Fox Television, *Steven Levitan Productions*, 2009.

Litman, Jessica. *Digital Copyright.* Amherst: Prometheus Books, 2006.

Lopez, German. "Why Amazon Spent $970 Million to Buy Twitch." *Vox*, August 26, 2014. https://www.vox.com/2014/8/26/6067085/amazon-twitch-tv-video-games-live-streaming-league-of-legends-dota-2.

LoPiccolo, Greg, Harmonix, and Ryan Lesser. Guitar Hero. Nintendo, PlayStation, Xbox. Boston: Harmonix, RedOctane, Activision, Aspyr, 2005.

LoPiccolo, Greg, Rob Kay, and Dan Teasdale. Rock Band. Xbox, PlayStation, Nintendo. Boston: Harmonix, MTV Games, 2007.

Lorenz, Taylor, Kellen Browning, and Sheera Frenkel. "TikTok Teens and K-Pop Stans Say They Sank Trump Rally." *The New York Times*, June 21, 2020, sec. Style. https://www.nytimes.com/2020/06/21/style/tiktok-trump-rally-tulsa.html.

Madden, John, Sony Interactive Entertainment LLC, and EA Sports (Firm). *Madden NFL 20*. English, 2019.

Marcuse, Herbert. *One-Dimensional Man: Studies in the Ideology of Advanced Industrial Society*. Boston: Beacon Press, 1991.

McLeod, Kembrew. "MP3s Are Killing Home Taping: The Rise of Internet Distribution and Its Challenge to the Major Label Music Monopoly." *Popular Music and Society* 28, no. 4 (October 2005): 521–31.

Mercuri, Monica. "Spotify Reports First Quarterly Operating Profit, Reaches 96 Million Paid Subscribers." *Forbes*, February 6, 2019, Online edition, sec. Hollywood & Entertainment. https://www.forbes.com/sites/monicamercuri/2019/02/06/spotify-reports-first-quarterly-operating-profit-reaches-96-million-paid-subscribers/.

Miller, Jennifer Lynn. "Diminished Citizenship: A Genealogy of the Development of 'Soft Citizenship' at the Intersection of US Mass and Political Culture." Dissertation, George Mason University, 2014. http://mars.gmu.edu/handle/1920/8857.

Miyamoto, Shigeru. Mario Kart. Nintendo. Kyoto, Japan: Nintendo, 1992.

Moaba, Alex. "Ann Romney Likes 'Modern Family,' But Show's Creator Pushes Back." *HuffPost*, August 28, 2012, Online edition, sec. TV & Film. https://www.huffpost.com/entry/modern-family-ann-romney_n_1837171.

Mosco, Vincent. *Becoming Digital: Toward a Post-Internet Society*. Bingley: Emerald Publishing Limited, 2017.

Mosco, Vincent. *The Pay-Per Society: Computers and Communication in the Information Age*. Norwood: Praeger, 1989.

Nieborg, David B. "Crushing Candy: The Free-to-Play Game in Its Connective Commodity Form." *Social Media + Society* 1, no. 2 (July 1, 2015): 2056305115621932. https://doi.org/10.1177/2056305115621932.

O'Leary, Nick. "Vimeo: YouTube's Better-Looking Little Brother." Medford: Information Today, Inc., November 2013.

Palm, Michael. *Technologies of Consumer Labor: A History of Self-Service*. New York: Routledge, 2016.

Palm, Michael. "Analog Backlog: Pressing Records during the Vinyl Revival." *Journal of Popular Music Studies* 29, no. 4 (December 1, 2017): n/a-n/a. https://doi.org/10.1111/jpms.12247.

Palm, Michael. "The New Old: Vinyl Records after the Internet." In *The Dialectic of Digital Culture*, edited by David Arditi and Jennifer Miller, 149–62. Lanham: Lexington Books, 2019.

Pardo, Rob, Jeff Kaplan, and Tom Chilton. *World of Warcraft*. Microsoft Windows, macOS. Irvine: Blizzard Entertainment, 2004.

Patry, William. *Moral Panics and the Copyright Wars*. New York: Oxford University Press, 2009.

Peele, Jordan. Get Out. Film. Universal Pictures, Blumhouse Productions, QC *Entertainment*, 2017.

Peoples, Glenn. "War of Words: Labels and Trade Groups Target YouTube's 'Value Gap.'" *Billboard*, April 13, 2016. http://www.billboard.com/articles/business/7333110/war-of-words-labels-trade-groups-youtube-value-gap.

Perzanowski, Aaron, and Jason Schultz. *The End of Ownership: Personal Property in the Digital Economy*. Cambridge: The MIT Press, 2016.

Prey, Robert. "Nothing Personal: Algorithmic Individuation on Music Streaming Platforms." *Media, Culture & Society* 40, no. 7 (October 1, 2018): 1086–1100. https://doi.org/10.1177/0163443717745147.

Putnam, Robert D. *Bowling Alone: The Collapse and Revival of American Community*. New York: Simon & Schuster, 2000. http://www.loc.gov/catdir/bios/simon054/00027278.html http://www.loc.gov/catdir/description/simon041/00027278.html http://www.loc.gov/catdir/enhancements/fy0705/00027278-t.html http://www.loc.gov/catdir/enhancements/fy0705/00027278-s.html.

Rosenthal, Andrew. "Bush Encounters the Supermarket, Amazed." *The New York Times*, February 5, 1992, sec. U.S. https://www.nytimes.com/1992/02/05/us/bush-encounters-the-supermarket-amazed.html.

Sandoval, Greg. "Mother Protects YouTube Clip by Suing Prince." *CNET*, October 30, 2007. http://news.cnet.com/8301-10784_3-9807555-7.html.

Shapter, Andrew. Before the Music Dies, 2006.

Should You Play WoW in 2020? – MMO Population Blog." Accessed August 4, 2020. https://mmo-population.com/blog/should-you-play-wow-in-2020/.

Smith Noah. "Racism, Misogyny, Death Threats: Why Can't the Booming Video-Game Industry Curb Toxicity?" *Washington Post*, February 26, 2019. https://www.washingtonpost.com/technology/2019/02/26/racism-misogyny-death-threats-why-cant-booming-video-game-industry-curb-toxicity/.

Smith, Paul. *Millennial Dreams: Contemporary Culture and Capital in the North. The Haymarket Series.* London; New York: Verso, 1997.

Smith, Paul. "Tommy Hilfiger in the Age of Mass Customization." In *No Sweat: Fashion, Free Trade, and the Rights of Garment Workers*, edited by Andrew Ross. London: Verso, 1997.

Smythe, Dallas Walker. "On the Audience Commodity and Its Work." In *Dependency Road: Communications, Capitalism, Consciousness, and Canada*, edited by Dallas Walker Smythe, 230–56. Norwood: Ablex, 1981.

Sony Corp. v. Universal City Studios, No. 81–1687 (United States Supreme Court January 17, 1984).

Spigel, Lynn. *Welcome to the Dreamhouse: Popular Media and Postwar Suburbs*. Durham: Duke University Press Books, 2001.

Srnicek, Nick. *Platform Capitalism*. Cambridge; Malden: Polity, 2017.

Stephen, Bijan. "Fortnite Showed Us the Future of Live Music (and Its Past, Too)." *The Verge*, February 18, 2019. https://www.theverge.com/2019/2/18/18229471/fortnite-marshmello-pleasant-park-live-music-future-past.

Sterne, Jonathan. *MP3: The Meaning of a Format*. Durham: Duke University Press, 2012.

Stewart, Dodai. "On Miley Cyrus, Ratchet Culture and Accessorizing With Black People." *Jezebel*, June 20, 2013. https://jezebel.com/on-miley-cyrus-ratchet-culture-and-accessorizing-with-514381016.

Taylor, T. L. *Watch Me Play: Twitch and the Rise of Game Live Streaming*. Princeton; Oxford: Princeton University Press, 2018.

Trust, Gary. "Imagine Dragons' 'Radioactive' Ends Record Billboard Hot 100 Run." *Billboard*, May 9, 2014. http://www.billboard.com/articles/columns/chart-beat/6084584/imagine-dragons-radioactive-ends-record-billboard-hot-100-run.

Tryon, Chuck. *On-Demand Culture: Digital Delivery and the Future of Movies*. None edition. New Brunswick: Rutgers University Press, 2013.

Turner, Graeme. "Television Studies, We Need to Talk about 'Binge-Viewing'." *Television & New Media*, September 26, 2019, 1527476419877041. https://doi.org/10.1177/1527476419877041.

Ugwu, Reggie. "The Hashtag That Changed the Oscars: An Oral History." *The New York Times*, February 6, 2020, sec. Movies. https://www.nytimes.com/2020/02/06/movies/oscarssowhite-history.html.

Wade, Peter. "Racism, Lies, and Empty Seats: The Embarrassment That Was Trump's Rally." *Rolling Stone*, June 21, 2020. https://www.rollingstone.com/politics/politics-news/racism-lies-empty-seats-the-embarrassment-that-was-trump-rally-1018329/.

Wareheim, Eric. "Indians on TV." Comedy. 3 Arts Entertainment, Alan Yang Pictures, Fremulon, 2015.

Watkins, S. Craig. *Hip Hop Matters: Politics, Pop Culture, and the Struggle for the Soul of a Movement*. Boston: Beacon Press, 2005.

Wells, Jason, and Megha Rajagopalan. "Trump Said He Plans To Ban TikTok From The US." *BuzzFeed News*, July 31, 2020. https://www.buzzfeednews.com/article/jasonwells/trump-plans-ban-tiktok-us.

Williams, Raymond. "'Culture Is Ordinary' (1958)." In *Resources of Hope: Culture, Democracy, Socialism*, 3–14. New York: Verso Books, 1989.

Williams, Raymond. "Moving from High Culture to Ordinary Culture." In *Convictions*, edited by N. McKenzie. London: MacGibbon & Kee, 1958.

Williams, Raymond. *Marxism and Literature*. Marxist Introductions. New York: Oxford University Press, 1977.

Williams, Raymond, and Ederyn Williams. *Television: Technology and Cultural Form*. *Routledge Classics*. London; New York: Routledge, 2003.

INDEX